A Legacy of Truth

March 20, 1993

To David —

In love + joy —

Kennedy Shultz

A LEGACY OF TRUTH

Great Minds
That Made Great Lives

J. Kennedy Shultz

DeVorss & Company, Publishers

FIRST DEVORSS & CO. EDITION, 1990

ISBN: 0-87516-622-9

DeVorss & Company, Publisher
P.O. Box 550
Marina del Rey, CA 90294

Printed in the United States of America

Contents

v

Across the disc of existence, each decade, there glide five hundred million souls, and disappear forever in the dim and dusk of the eternity that lies behind. Out of the bare handful that are remembered, we cherish only the memory of those who stood alone and expressed their honest, inmost thought. And this thought is, always and forever, the thought of liberty. Future generations often confuse these men with Deity, the Maker of the Worlds—for in fact these men were Sons of God, vitalized by Divinity, part and parcel of the power that guides the planets on their way and holds the worlds in space. Upon their tombs we carve a single word: SAVIOR.

—Elbert Hubbard

Preface

There is within each of us an unending desire to be greater than we presently are. This is true of people who have already achieved much success and people who have not. Because our possibilities are endless, something within us always knows that and announces it to us by means of our endless desiring. This is not a cruel and unreasonable demanding. It is good news. It is a true sign of life.

Life cannot go on unless it is moving forward. It intends to move forward in us, but will move forward without us if necessary. If we will not find within ourselves a way to let this happen, life must abandon us through a process of disintegration. This process occurs sometimes quickly and other times with painful and debilitating slowness. But it is always reversible if we can find a way to bring ourselves into a consciousness of receptivity to new and greater ideas concerning life and our part in it.

Great lives are the products of great minds. Great minds are created by receptivity to great new ideas and personal commitment to pursue them passionately. Ideas are great when they support life-giving, life-healing concepts as universally available, applicable, and desirable.

They are always simple concepts about such things as individual freedom, universal peace, unconditional love, and ever-expanding productivity.

Such ideas give renewed life to one and all. They are the stuff that has let the human race come to live better and better over the eons of our existence. Such ideas have been re-introduced and professed anew in every generation by enough individuals to keep human life in this world moving forward, if ever so slowly, in spite of all the ignorance and cruelty that has plagued every age.

Most of these good souls achieved no great fame in their time and will never be known to us. There is nothing wrong with that. It is exactly as it should be. They made their point, gave their gift, and went on their way. Their contributions flourish in the eternal and silent consciousness we all share, coming forth into the awareness of all who seek enlightenment in any age. These multitudes who have done their good and gone their way were yesterday's wise and loving mothers and fathers, grandmas and grandpas, uncles, aunts, loyal friends, and devoted teachers.

As such good people existed in the past, they also exist in the present. They are in our homes and workplaces, and all about wherever people are living with people. You will find them when you become interested in what they are about. They are never people feeding on ego or championing a cause. They are not people promoting a sect or defining a theology. They are simply individuals living serenely, loving quietly, and responding gently and wisely to their environment. If this were not so, and if it had not always been so, our race would have extinguished itself ages ago. For life will not support that which does not, for the most part, fulfill its creative intention of continued growth and expansion in all good things.

In every age some of these lovers of life and seekers of truth have risen to stardom. Their particular nature has not permitted them the security and peace of anonymity. Their fame has carried their names and their particular contributions down through the centuries. Each one represents to us today the greatest thinking of his or her age. We call them heroes and heroines because their lives required much courage and sometimes great sacrifice. But none thought himself heroic. Each did only what his nature dictated. There was no real choice. Sometimes we call them saviors. But they saved no one, if by salvation we mean making it possible for any of us to get any more than we can make ourselves worthy of by our own endeavors. None of them saved themselves from this necessity either.

They were neither heroes nor saviors in the usual sense of these words. They were more than all that. They were ordinary people who decided to live according to extraordinary ideas and who consequently provided all around them, and all who would come after them, a way to improve their livingness and the life of our world on the whole. Their consciousness became our treasured legacy, a legacy of truth.

For this book I have selected twelve such individuals to write about from a field which includes many more. This does not suggest that I consider these the greatest. It is simply that, at this point in time, these twelve compel my greatest interest. Each is taken from a different era and is a very different kind of person from the others. As people they have little in common. Each one loved the knowable more than the known. Each one knew that the knowable was knowable only to the knower. Each was committed to make right knowers of us all, and fervently believed this was possible.

Only in thought were they alike. In particulars they were stunningly different. But thought is the medium through which we all relate meaningfully to each other. It is our common creator.

And so we have Socrates, with the physique and strength of a bull, thinking right along with puny, misshapen Immanuel Kant. And Socrates, the professional pauper, sharing common ideas with the rich and elegant Swedenborg. The austere and certainly celibate Meister Eckhart speaks the same truth as Voltaire, the comfort-loving wit and notorious womanizer. Marcus Aurelius, all-powerful emperor of Rome, and Spinoza, the outcast Jew of Amsterdam and humble lens-grinder, looked at life through the same eyes. Herbert Spencer, the friendless bachelor and denizen of cheap London boarding houses, revelled in the magnificence of the cosmos right along with the aristocratic, pleasure-loving Lucretius. And the gentle Schweitzer, whose science of love led him to great acts of mercy, was at perfect ease with the ideas of Giordano Bruno, whose great love of science led him to merciless torment.

I offer this book about these twelve extraordinary men to all those who recognize within themselves the urgent desire to be more than they now appear to be. I offer it to help them understand the rightness of this desire and to realize the direction they must take to fulfill it. The direction is always inward. The commitment is always personal. And the reward is always an ever-expanding life of integrity and joy and abundance. This book is not intended to be a scholarly work, but an easy read. There are enough scholarly works already in circulation, and out of circulation, about these twelve individuals that are not being read. What I have to say in this book about their lives and works is easily verifiable in any good public library. My conclusions are, of course, my own and can only be verified in the consciousness of each reader. If they make sense to you, you are welcome to them. If they do not, I encourage you to look elsewhere with all my blessing.

KENNEDY SHULTZ
Atlanta, Georgia

A Legacy of Truth

1

Midwife to the Mind

Socrates
(470–399 B.C.)

MORE THAN 400 years before Jesus trod the dusty roads of Judea preaching his gospel of salvation from within, Socrates plodded about the streets of Athens teaching that the only real knowledge is self-knowledge. We will learn, he contended, only when we persist in asking ourselves the questions we so urgently wish to have answered by others.

Few people listened to either Socrates or Jesus, and even fewer heard what they had to say. People do not easily accept personal responsibility for their own betterment. Human resistance to this is deeply programmed and is both strong and incredibly devious. So devious that people find it easy to sincerely believe they are looking within and perceiving great new understanding, when all they are really doing is responding passionately to the ideas of another. They become the kind of people who are ready

3

to lie down and die for someone else's beliefs, but never quite able to stand up and live by their own. The world has always had a lot of such people and has suffered greatly from their mischief.

Both Socrates and Jesus were master teachers, not mere instructors or propagandizers. Neither wanted to impose ideas or give ready-made answers. Both wanted to teach people *how* to think, not *what* to think, because both had unfaltering faith in the creative power of the human mind in every person. Socrates said, "Character is a matter of growth, and all I hope to do is to make you think for yourselves."

Wisdom cannot be imported. We will not find it lying in wait for us even in the greatest books ever written. Whatever we read or hear must be taken into our minds and questioned over and over again, before we will discover what is really so. And when we really know, we will know that we know and not be burdened by the need to defend it or force it upon others. So the reward for wisdom is peace of mind and effectiveness in living in the world around us. We will be able to go ahead and live without needing too much praise or shrinking too much from fear of criticism.

Both Jesus and Socrates were generally despised in their lifetimes. Most people hate challenges to their habitual belief systems, even if those belief systems have never worked very well. Persons who persistently challenge them will always get into serious trouble. And they are revolutionaries of the most feared sort—revolutionaries of the mind. If we allow our thinking to be revolutionized, then many of the most cherished structures of our lives will surely come tumbling down, and we will have more of a reconstruction job on our hands than most people are willing to face.

People really don't want change. They want comfort. And there is no greater comfort than believing that one is already right about everything. We are willing to give up much for this kind of comfort, including our happiness and our creativity. That is why most people spend much more time and energy justifying their limitations than trying to overcome them. The most popular way of doing this is to blame them on God, or life (as in "That's life"), or to blame them on other people. This clears the way for us to practice either passionate grief or seething resentment. Both of which provide excellent ways of blowing off steam while at the same time avoiding the necessity of change.

At the time of Jesus the Jews had gotten so used to waiting for their Messiah, they had forgotten how to do anything but wait, and weep, and suffer. They really didn't want a Messiah. They wanted to be comforted and catered to for *not* having a Messiah. If a Messiah actually came along, he would spoil the whole scheme. They could never put up with that. And indeed, they didn't.

The Athenians in Socrates' day had gotten so used to going to their sacred oracles and paying cash for quick answers, the idea of sitting still and probing their own consciousness for their greater good was odious to them. It would require more patience than they cared to invest; it would deprive them of pious ceremony they had come to adore; and, of course, it would force them to reject a traditional mentality carefully constructed upon many years of limited thinking.

So both Jesus and Socrates were generally ignored and

despised in their own lifetimes. But each of them was heard and loved by a few. And from the devotion of these few their great wisdom has come down through the centuries to be heard by the few in every age who have ears to hear. It is these few in every age who have kept the world rolling forward in the face of the cruel nonsense of the many.

The wisdom of Jesus has never been widely embraced, not even by the part of the world that calls itself Christian. Likewise, the wisdom of Socrates has led only a few great minds in every age to greater understanding. Most people are traditionally caught up in other things, like making a buck, looking good, and wondering who's to blame for their endless dissatisfaction.

Socrates was the son of a stonemason and a midwife. He was expected, as sons often are, to follow in his father's footsteps. It seemed that he would do this. He took up the tools of the stonemason's trade as a young man, but his life did not really begin until he laid them down once and for all at the age of thirty-five. He may have been a good craftsman, but he seems not to have been a very productive one, because he could not keep his nose to the grindstone. He was too busy sticking it into other people's business, always ready to lay down his tools and enter into lengthy discussions with anyone who would talk to him about anything he could get them to talk about.

He had a deep and compelling thirst for knowledge. He was convinced he knew nothing, although everybody else seemed sure they knew something. He wanted to know what they knew. And so he questioned them endlessly. His manner was argumentative, but not for the sake of argument. It was just that he couldn't accept their knowledge unless he could justify it.

His years as a stonemason gave him a strong and muscular physique—as bull-like as his manner. This served him well when he became a professional antagonist. A slighter man might not have been able to push so hard and get away with it without being knocked down a time or two.

He would stop the wise men of Athens in the street and demand to know what they thought about everything and then challenge their justification for their thinking. He soon learned that all of them, like himself, really knew nothing for sure.

This led him to believe that one cannot really know anything but oneself—one's own mind and heart: How one thinks, how one feels, how one acts and reacts, and whether all of that is really productive of the kind of experience one seeks. Real wisdom, he concluded, was in bringing one's thoughts and feelings, one's actions and reactions, into harmony with Nature. This became the foundation of his philosophy and the essence of his teaching. Though he set out to be only a learner, he wound up being a teacher whose first and only commandment was "Know thyself," and whose only dictum was "The unexamined life is not worth living."

So Socrates did not follow in his father's footsteps, but in a strange way this burly, bald, bow-legged man followed in his mother's footsteps. He often described himself as a midwife to the mind, helping others give birth to their own ideas by guiding them through the painful and laborious process of probing their own consciousness, and drawing forth their own conclusions. So that in the end, this process would give birth to a whole new person.

His students did not come in droves, but over the course of his long life they came in a steady stream from all places, all social classes, and for many different reasons. Gathered round him at any given time were the rich and the poor, the old and the young, the humble and the haughty.

The enormously wealthy Crito came to Socrates to learn how to get the happiness that money and power could not command. Euclid of Megara was nearly eighty when he came to Socrates to learn how to heal his bad temper and sharp tongue. Aeschines, an ambitious young man who could never get enough, came to very gratefully learn how truly happy he could be with far less.

Perhaps his most famous students were two very dissimilar characters, the heroic Alcibiades and the immortal Plato. Each came to draw from within himself his own special kind of greatness.

Alcibiades was an unlikely candidate for wisdom. At age twenty-one he came to Socrates as a thoroughly spoiled brat. He was considered the handsomest man in Athens and the rudest. His family was very rich and very well-connected. He was proud and insolent, given to outrageous behavior in public and towards his friends in private. Wealth and beauty protected him from any reprisals from without and his upbringing deprived him of any real discipline from within. He was a young god run riot.

This arrogant young man came to Socrates the first time intent on disrupting his little assembly with his celebrated wit. Socrates quickly made a total fool out of him in front of all the others. It is always dangerous to expose a fool as a fool, and Alcibiades responded to this outrage by getting physical with the old man. He challenged Socrates to wrestle. The challenge was quickly accepted and in less time than it took to devastate the young man with words, Socrates had him pinned to the mat.

From that moment Alcibiades was devoted to Socrates for life. Though the young man had no great capacity for philosophy, he did learn at Socrates' feet how to become a decent human being, a model citizen, and a great hero of Athens.

Alcibiades gave Socrates something to be proud of, but Plato gave him much more. Plato, or at least his philosophy, gave Socrates immortality.

It is through the writings of Plato that we know of Socrates today. And it is because of the influence of Socrates that Plato is hailed to this day as the world's most complete philosopher. "Say what you will, you'll find it all in Plato," wrote Emerson. Many others have observed that if Socrates had done nothing more than give shape to the mind of Plato, he would deserve the world's eternal gratitude.

Plato was twenty when he came to Socrates. The old man was sixty. It was love at first sight, and for the next fifty years Plato devoted himself to recording the dialogues of Socrates and presenting Socrates' teaching with an eloquence and clarity that is the hallmark of his own genius.

Plato's love for Socrates was the love of genius beholding genius. It had nothing to do with personality, manner, or style. The two men could not have been more dissimilar on that level. Plato was a wealthy, refined, pleasure-seeking youth of Athens. His manners were elegant, his appearance fastidious. He had the intellect to appreciate the genius of Socrates endlessly and the character to never even consider imitating him in any way. He never confused Socrates' determined poverty, rough and ready manner, or slovenly appearance with his genius. It has been said that imitation is the highest form of flattery.

Plato was neither flatterer nor imitator. He honored Socrates not by becoming more like him, but by becoming more and more like himself.

Through Plato we look into the heart of Socrates. He explains much, including the Socratic idea of objective scrutiny as a means of knowing one's self. This is the self-developed ability to mentally step outside of ourselves and take a look at what is really going on in our lives—what we are really doing, how we are really thinking and feeling—judging for ourselves if it is all really productive. If we find ourselves operating in anger or confusion or fear, we know immediately we are wrong and some adjustment is called for. These things are not natural to life, can never be justified, and will never produce good results. The action required is not to denounce ourselves, but to renounce this activity for ourselves, because otherwise we will never learn to operate more productively.

Plato also tells us that Socrates' greatest desire was to live beyond desire. He believed this was the only way to live in peace. Living beyond desire does not mean having no desire. That is both impossible and unnatural. It means knowing how to live well before our desires are fulfilled, after they are fulfilled, and whether or not any particular desire is ever fulfilled. Everything that is necessary to a good life, Socrates taught, will come around to us if we stop projecting negativity into our environment. The only demands we have any right to make are upon ourselves to produce a better nature. We have no right to demand that others fulfill our expectations, and we have no obligation to allow others to force us to fulfill theirs.

Socrates held these principles to be universal. They were true for everyone. They could profitably be applied by all, under all conditions. Though religions and cultures are many and diverse, he taught that goodness and kindness are forever one. And goodness and kindness demand that we respect and encourage all people to pursue wisdom in their own way.

In Socrates' time there was as much speculation about the hereafter as there is today. There was also as much superstition. Socrates sensed the immortality of the soul and certainly believed in a life beyond our mortal existence. But he warned against hoping to have our problems solved and our characters cleansed at some future time. The highest wisdom is to live as well as we can in the here and now, he taught. This is the only intelligent preparation for whatever is to come.

From Plato we discover that this is how Socrates conducted hismelf during his long life and how he conducted himself at the end of it. His credibility was ultimately established through his courage.

Socrates' many years of questioning the great leaders of Athens and thereby exposing their stupidities and selfishness made him a dangerous character. The young men who studied with him, and who in their turn responded to established authority in the same way, brought even more official displeasure down on his head. The establishment wanted to silence this outrageous old man. They brought him to trial on charges of treason to the state by questioning the wisdom of the gods and corrupting the youth of Athens by encouraging them to do the same. They did not want to kill him, only frighten him into silence. They offered a confession for him to read at his trial, including a promise to teach no more. He refused it and instead insisted on conducting his own defense, which he did with devastating eloquence. He made it clear that he had no disrespect for the gods, only for venal men who thought they were gods. As we said earlier, it is always dangerous to make fools of fools. So he was convicted and sentenced to die by drinking hemlock.

When the time came for him to take the fatal cup, his closest friends gathered in his room to comfort him. It was, however, Socrates who comforted them. He reminded them in their grief that his life was not ending, but moving on to a better experience, and that they could best honor him not by mourning him but by always seeking to improve the conduct of their own lives.

These are the words of a man who knows and who knows that he knows. And what he knew he learned at his own expense and taught at his own expense as well.

Four centuries later another man called Jesus came along, abandoned the work the world had cut out for him to do, and went about preaching and teaching the very same principles. We do not know that Jesus ever heard of Socrates, and we can be rather sure that he never read Plato. But Socrates had no Socrates to follow, and Plato had no Plato to read. And so Jesus proved the wisdom of Socrates by drawing from within the bosom of his own consciousness a personal understanding of the principles that Socrates had found within himself. And like Socrates, Jesus was compelled to both preach and practice them with conviction and eloquence. The world was no more ready to hear them than it had been four hundred years earlier. It is still not ready to hear them today. That, however, should not be viewed as a tragedy. Because this wisdom is not for the world. It is for people who are tired of the world, tired of trying to find their good in their environment, and who are willing to bring more good into their environment. It is for people who want to change themselves in the world and so change the world they live in.

Each of these men accomplished this in themselves and in their time. Each also left a permanent legacy of truth to prick the consciousness of people in following ages and to urge them to pursue their inner greatness and produce their own greater livingness.

Of the two, Socrates remains the more influential. Because, up to this time at least, he is less misunderstood than Jesus. The world has not decided to use Socrates as its hero and its authority to pursue its own purposes. Therefore his words have not been twisted, his nature not distorted, his biography not loaded with absurdities. No crimes have been committed in his name, no wars waged, limitations justified or sickness explained away as his will. No absurd and impractical theology has been devised on his supposed authority. No one has abused his credibility in order to establish theirs.

Jesus deserves far better than this, and we deserve a far better understanding of Jesus than has been handed down to us. But any individual who has ears to hear or eyes to see and is willing to pursue his own greater wisdom within himself will find it anyway, and will be able to see as these great men saw, live with their same freedom and serenity, and when the time comes to die to this world, to look forward with certainty to a new life beyond it.

2

Pre-Scientist of Rome

Lucretius
(96–55 B.C.)

THERE IS NO profit where no pleasure is taken," wrote the great Plato. This is an astonishing statement. He is actually saying that life is for pleasure. Unless we can enjoy living, there is no good reason for staying alive, let alone trying to make something out of our lives. This concept flies in the face of the age-old belief that our life on this earth is for proving ourselves worthy of a better life in the hereafter, a painful struggle towards a rather nebulous future. This kind of thought has made a virtue out of suffering and has led us to believe we are doing good when we are feeling bad about what we are doing or missing out on. If our efforts are not tiring, frustrating, and in danger of failure, they really can't produce anything of value. If we find things too easy or actually take pleasure in our own endeavors, they don't count as much and will create nothing of lasting value.

In pagan times pleasure was the prerogative of the gods. They flew about through the cosmos having their way with each other and in all things on earth. All this while humans struggled along, condemned to hardship because of their gross humanity. Occasionally the gods would dispense some small favor as payment for service or sacrifice. But for the most part a person could only hope that some day when his or her days of toil on earth were done he or she would be lifted up among the gods to partake in a life of eternal pleasure.

This primitive, pagan line of thought was adopted by the emerging Christian church and incorporated into its theology. It was thereafter used to explain away life's misery rather than to deal with the challenge of healing it. It was also used to keep people working themselves to death for little earthly reward, obeying the oppressive laws of both church and state without challenge, and blindly professing to believe in ideas that served them poorly and defied common sense.

Pleasure came to be a shameful thing. One could not seek to enjoy life without risking mortal peril. The idea was to suffer now and rejoice later. That is why our traditional idea of heaven is a place where we will be exempt from every kind of energetic output. We won't even have to walk, just float around. There will certainly be no heavy lifting. In heaven unemployment is not a disgrace but the natural order of things. We will not work for our daily bread because we will either exist beyond hunger or have nectar and ambrosia poured down our waiting gullets by angel hands. As far as sex is concerned, like the gods and goddesses of the ancients, we will either be entirely free to have as much as we want with anyone we choose, or we won't want it at all. This latter option has great appeal to modern Christians, whose sexual guilt has made sexuality more of a problem than a pleasure anyhow.

Our civilization has come to terms with Plato, and his belief in the profitability of pleasure, by misinterpreting him. We are taught that he was speaking only of the joys of the spiritual life, not earthly pleasures. We have coined the term *platonic* and use it to mean nonphysical or having no physical fulfillment. More specifically, it has come to mean nonsexual. So that platonic love, for example, is love without sex. And platonic love is more noble than love that finds expression through sexual activity. But Plato was both a loving and highly sexual man. He took great pleasure in his sexuality throughout his long life. His sex life was a great deal more active and more varied than most people today care to acknowledge.

To Plato, love, like all human activity, was platonic not when it was nonphysical but when it was expressed with joy and dignity and for good purpose; that is, when it was expressed with pleasure and for profit.

Lucretius spoke even more clearly about the rightness of pleasure. He said that pleasure is the purpose of human life. To him, a life without pleasure was a life wasted. True pleasure, he reasoned, could be achieved only through a consciousness of peace and a pure heart. All the physical senses were to be employed in the expression of pleasure and all the physical appetites fully satisfied. But the ways in which we achieved this had to be ways that were healthful to ourselves and beneficial to our fellow beings. Lucretius was influenced by a school of thought named after the Roman philosopher Epicurus.

The pious pagan religionists of ancient Rome despised the Epicurean philosophy. They made *epicurean* a dirty word to be hurled at every kind of excessive behavior. The word comes down to us as meaning a selfish interest in satisfying physical appetites. At best it means delighting in food and drink. At worst it implies mindless gluttony.

Titus Lucretius Carus was a Roman aristocrat. He lived well and labored little, leaving behind only one work to testify to the greatness of his mind. It is a long epic poem concerning the creation of the universe and the meaning of life in the world. It is called *On the Nature of Things.* This highly colorful piece has had a tremendous impact on great minds in every age. Walt Whitman found in it the seed of his concept of spiritual democracy. Albert Einstein found it of such merit that he wrote the introduction to a modern German translation.

While Lucretius' conclusions about the rightness of every kind of pleasure are both delightful and interesting, the essential philosophy that led him to such conclusions is astonishing for its depth of insight and greatness of spirit.

Writing a century before the birth of Jesus and much longer before the emergence of modern scientific thought, Lucretius described the universe as being created out of a cosmic chaos that produced its own order based upon a law of its own nature. So the universe was not fashioned to perfection by the hand of an unseen entity and presented to us as a riddle to be worked out at the peril of our immortal souls. It was, rather, a logical and creative system entirely knowable by all people as all people are themselves a part of this system. People who will take the time and patience to detect the way life works in the universe, according to Lucretius, will be able to let it so work for them in their individual lives. In this manner they will create a life experience for themselves that is personally pleasurable and a joy to behold. Such people will not only rise up as good examples to the rest of the world, but will produce offspring who will go on to develop even greater insights into life and create even more successful and productive life experiences. The future then would be shaped by those who understood the universe and lived by its laws.

Lucretius said the physical universe consisted of atoms, motion, and void. The atoms had fixed qualities themselves but could combine in an infinite variety of ways to produce the appearance of an infinite variety of structures or things. The law that governed how the atoms would combine, he theorized, is a law of motion. So the atoms, the basic building blocks of all things, are in continuous motion, creating and maintaining an infinity of things, and by the same law of motion, changing and eventually obliterating all things. The void, wrote Lucretius, was the medium or ether through which the atoms move in order to create form. Because of the nature of the creative law, nothing on the physical plane of existence is permanent. Everything integrates and then disintegrates, so that all is eternally passing from the invisible into the visible then back into the invisible again to give itself up to the life process of eternal renewal.

Lucretius included the human body as one of the things that come and go in the natural process of life. He extended his theory to the human psyche or individual personality as well. He believed that, like the body, the individual personality that is tailored to it also disintegrates and reemerges as part of the re-creation of some other form.

Death, then, is both natural and inevitable. So there is nothing to fear from it and little sense in worrying about it. It is not an end of anything. It is a process of the transformation of life in which we are changed but never diminished.

The purpose of life, according to Lucretius, is to have a good time living it, for as they say, we will never pass this way again. This does not mean we are to dash about in wild abandon, mindlessly entertaining ourselves and satisfying all our bodily appetites, come what may. This would not be constructive, and so would be entirely inconsistent with the laws of life, which always creates cosmos out of chaos, not the reverse.

What Lucretius would have us do to find the greatest pleasure in life is to make ourselves a joyful and harmonious expression of the universe—enjoying life by adding to it, revelling in beauty by being beautiful, prospering by giving our best, and finding every kind of pleasure by giving every kind of pleasure to others. In other words, to live primarily as creator, rather than primarily as consumer. Lucretius certainly believed pleasure to be the purpose of life, but real pleasure can be experienced only by the pure of heart, the generous soul, and the clear mind.

Real pleasure never violates personal integrity. This includes personal health of body, soul, or mind of any person. Pleasure, joy, is the nature of true divinity, not a snare of some imaginary devil.

Roman religion at the time of Lucretius was based upon an endlessly complex theology of gods and goddesses for all purposes and frequently at cross-purposes.

It had become highly structured, severely formalized, and unrealistically demanding in an hysterical way, rather like a rejected wife who knows no one cares any more but is determined to have her due, or else. Those trying to uphold, or rather hold up, this sagging system branded Lucretius an atheist. Religious bigots throughout history label as atheist anyone who awakens in them disturbing doubts about their sectarian doctrines. The word *atheist* means not believing in God or a Supreme Creative Power. It does not mean rejecting invented doctrines, creeds, or forms of religious observance. All of these came after God, not before or along with.

Actually Lucretius never went so far as to deny the existence of the Roman gods. He did, however, deny them power over human existence. He said the mighty gods and goddesses of Rome existed somewhere out in the void in the spaces between the life-giving atoms and somewhere beyond the creative law of motion. Whoever they were, and whatever and wherever they were, they had no interest in our lives or any influence over our livingness. It was, therefore, rather foolish to get all caught up in devotions and rituals to implore their guidance and curry their favor. There is a power that will guide us right, Lucretius argued, but it comes from beyond the gods. And it comes to each one of us directly, filling our hearts and minds with its wisdom and strength that we might, as Jesus later said, have life abundant.

Many centuries earlier, Moses had come down from the mountain to tell his followers that there is only one God. They liked the idea, even though they didn't quite get it. The pious pagans of Rome didn't get it either. And if you really want to look at it closely, most people and most modern religions still don't get it. Many Christian sects are still largely obsessed with saints and angels. The Jewish religion has become very much a thing of culture and ritual. And all pious folks are obsessed with the devil or some form of external evil force which, of course, is merely a negative god. The totally irreligious are often given to materialism and to personal satisfaction in the acquisition of status and things.

And nobody's having much fun!

Some of our greatest spiritual minds have taken exception to Lucretius' idea that the individual personality disintegrates with the body. They reason that the personality is what we have made of the soul in our lifetime. And that since both the soul and the personality are not attached to the body—that is, are not physical—there is no reason to conclude that the soul does not continue to express and refine personality after physical death.

This is a very hopeful idea and certainly a very logical one. But we can easily see that it is an idea that comes about from an interest in Lucretius, not an out-of-hand rejection of his work. It is not an idea of a mind rooted in superstition, but a consciousness seeking greater knowledge.

We can expect to reemerge in the physical world in a new form if we choose to believe that. We can settle for the idea of death as simply non-being if we find that reasonable. But unless we can order our minds and hearts in the production of a life that can be lived with both honor and pleasure right here and right now, we will have little to take along with us, or little to leave behind.

3

Divine Emperor
Marcus Aurelius
(121–180)

Everything harmonizes with me which is harmonious to thee, O Universe. Nothing for me is too early or too late which is in due time for thee. Everything is fruit to me which thy seasons bring, O Nature: from thee are all things, in thee are all things, to thee are all things.

THIS IS THE prayer of Marcus Aurelius, Emperor of Rome. It is the ultimate "thy will be done" prayer expressed by a consciousness of total faith in the one perfect goodness and givingness of the Infinite.

Marcus Aurelius presided over an empire with an ancient state religion which would not sanction and could not inspire such a prayer. It was a religion with a wide array of gods and goddesses, each assigned dominion over some phase of life-giving or life-enhancing activity. These were supernatural entities that had to magically bend the rules in order to give the poor supplicant what he prayed for, which was usually more than he thought he deserved. Prayer to these supernatural beings was a matter of prescribed ritual, frequently involving some sort of sacrifice. It was designed to plead with them, to please them, to win them over to one's cause. It was superstitious prayer.

This noble prayer of Marcus Aurelius is nothing like that at all. It is an affirmation of faith in one supreme creative source. It asks for nothing. It expresses a perfect ability and willingness to find in all things of life a way to flourish. It is predicated upon a belief in a god-power that is natural and always life-giving in natural ways. The purpose of this prayer is not to bend the will of the gods to the will of the man. It is to elevate the human mind to the realization of the universal and eternal goodness of One God. Instead of trying to drag the gods down into the troubles of the world, this kind of prayer is designed to lift the individual consciousness up out of the troubles of the world to a point of realization that there is a life beyond our difficulties. It is a life that begins for us when we raise our consciousness to greater ideas.

As Emperor of Rome, Marcus Aurelius was under obligation to preserve and defend both the empire and its state religion. He did this vigorously against all outside threats, including the political threat presented by Christianity. He found in early Christianity as much superstition as in the old religion of Rome. It offered nothing really new except the imposition of a new and foreign god, and it was not so much dedicated to raising the spiritual consciousness of the people as it was to grasping temporal power for its leaders. In other words, it would disturb the ancient order without improving the well-being of the empire and its people.

As Emperor, Marcus Aurelius was the final authority on all things in Rome, both temporal and religious. His thought was far in advance of the traditional attitudes of his people. But he was a humble man as well as a wise one. He knew that good leadership must always see beyond, but can never force people to move beyond, their traditional beliefs and affections. They can be led, but they cannot be driven. Any leader so intoxicated by his power that he tries to drive them will only drive himself out of control, because the power to rule always comes from the people being ruled.

His purpose was to lead, not coerce. And lead he did. He was powerful enough to plainly announce that his prayer of affirmation was the only sensible way to pray. But he was wise and humble enough to allow those who did not have the faith to utter this kind of prayer the right to pray as best they could.

Most people still don't have the faith to pray this way. This is because most people do not see God as the natural universal giver of all good. Our attitude towards God is still pagan. It projects a belief in a supernatural power that may or may not respond to us, that holds grudges, plays favorites, and sends us suffering and limitation to punish us, test us, or teach us lessons. Our prayer must then be designed to win God's good will. We do that by praise, or by assuming a position or engaging in rituals which we are told are particularly pleasing to God. We no longer sacrifice bulls or doves, but we do offer sacrifice. We promise to give up this pleasure or that, as if our personal deprivation is somehow pleasing to God, as if God finds delight when we give up ice cream or cigarettes or ball games or sex. We approach the Infinite as if God were some peevish taskmaster in the sky who has to be cajoled into giving us the fullness of life.

Marcus Aurelius was way ahead of us. He is still way ahead of a great number of our religious leaders who have a very small-minded view of God and a very superstitious approach to prayer. In our day, as in the days of Marcus Aurelius, such a view prevails. That is why, after all our centuries of progress, most people get very little out of life and pay a great deal for it. Today, as of old, most people are poor, succumb to terrible illness, work hard and get little, give much and end up alone. And what is worse, most people live their entire life with more unhappiness than happiness. For the average individual, life really is a "vale of sorrow," only because their consciousness is earthbound. For all their pious religiosity, they never appreciate the greatness and goodness of God and never engage in the kind of prayer that will lift them up to this vision. And that's a great pity, because what we need to know is knowable. Marcus Aurelius knew it, Jesus knew it, and many, many people before and since have known it. There are people all around us today who, in their own way, know it. They are not the ones who are trying to force their views upon you. They are the ones who are living well, loving much, and letting you and me be free to do the same in our own way.

The future Emperor of Rome was not born to royalty. In fact, he did not have a Roman pedigree. His family were Spaniards who had served Rome with distinction for many years, and had prospered. Hadrian, who was emperor through the years of Marcus' youth, was also a Spaniard. This made being Spanish an "in" thing, but still it was no substitute for being a Roman blueblood.

He was born Marcus Verus. His father died when the boy was very young. By good fortune he was sent to live in Rome with his rich and much honored grandfather, Annius Verus. The old man had been a soldier, a provincial governor, a judge, a senator, and a consul of Rome. But now he was retired, and with great delight he received his little grandson and set out to give him the best sort of upbringing and education his money could buy and his wealth of experience could inspire.

The child was a good and grateful student, and a dutiful grandson. With the years the bond between them grew strong and sweet. Young Marcus Verus grew to be an excellent young man. The Emperor Hadrian was a frequent visitor at the villa of Annius Verus. He became immensely fond of Marcus and impressed by his ability. When Marcus was the right age, Hadrian saw that he was put to work in government. The young man continued to excel and to grow in Hadrian's favor, so much so that the childless emperor saw to it that Marcus was legally placed in the line of succession to the throne.

At the age of forty Marcus ascended the throne, assuming the name of Aurelius in honor of his uncle who had ruled just before him. Marcus Aurelius became Emperor of Rome not without considerable political help, but without bloodshed or even serious challenge, which was quite an achievement in those days of unbridled ambition and seething intrigue.

At this time in Rome the emperor was the supreme authority in all things. He headed the administration, commanded the army, approved religious practice, and acted as chief magistrate. In this last capacity he was sort of a one-man Supreme Court. Marcus Aurelius served with distinction in all these capacities. However, his great vision and his love of justice are best reflected in his judicial decisions, many of which were revolutionary.

Although they were revolutionary, they were given only when he knew the people themselves were ripe for revolution. They were revolutionary on the side of giving people more latitude in the running of their own affairs. He believed in removing government regulations to the degree people could be responsible for setting their own standards and arranging their own justice. His object was to perceive what the people thought was right and then legalize it. This, of course, implies a respect for human intelligence and a belief that it should be encouraged.

In those days, as today, the courts were clogged with all sorts of lawsuits. People grew more and more contentious, and lawyers grew richer and richer. People dragged each other to court on the slightest provocation. They were not seeking justice. They were seeking to fleece each other on whatever pretext. The courts became overburdened and therefore corrupt. Society became confused and unstable.

Marcus believed that people should be discouraged from abusing the law with false claims and, in the case of just disputes, encouraged to settle their differences privately if at all possible. Again we see his belief in the intelligence of the individual. To encourage this, he ruled that all direct taxes would be remitted to every citizen who had not been the plaintiff in a lawsuit for ten years. This is a wonderful example of effective government by rewarding for good effort rather than punishing for wrongdoing. It is always less expensive to give rewards than to impose punishments. In the long run, it is more effective as well.

Furthermore, to encourage people to deal reasonably and fairly with other people is consistent with the highest good of all. Marcus expressed it this way:

We are made for cooperation, like feet, like hands, like eyelids, like rows of upper and lower teeth. To act against one another, then, is contrary to nature, and it is acting against each other to be vexed and turn away.

If in vexation we turn away and turn others loose, in this case lawyers and judges, to settle our disputes, we are failing to recognize our own natural purpose and to exercise our own natural responsibility. No one grows or truly profits from this tendency.

At one point during his rule, it became the fashion to cohabitate without marriage. They did not have pills and other devices to prevent unwanted pregnancies as we do today, so there were an increasing number of illegitimate children being produced. This was perhaps a greater problem in ancient Rome than it is today, for so much was based upon class, title, property, and the right to citizenship. Marcus would have made all children legitimate by right of birth. He disliked the stigma of illegitimacy. He wrote, "All children are blessings sent by the gods." In his mind it was unfair to punish them for the circumstances of their birth, and unprofitable for society as well.

Properly married people objected to making the children of the unwed legitimate. They claimed it would be the same as doing away with the sacred institution of marriage. In answer to this, the wise emperor simply redefined marriage: He ruled that all people are married who say they are, and all their children are therefore fully legitimate. In this decision by Marcus Aurelius we find the roots of our common-law marriage as it exists in the world today. It is still not respectable, of course, to "properly married" folks, but the children of such unions do have the full protection of the law.

Up to the time of the reign of Marcus Aurelius, husbands could get rid of their wives at will and also be absolved of all responsibility to support them. The husband had only to file his intention and the deed was done. Marcus sensed the terrible injustice in this. He was also aware of its negative impact on society, turning women loose with nowhere to go and no way to live. Rome, in his opinion, was too great to permit this inhumanity and very poorly served by people thrust into poverty and degradation.

Under his rule, the husband filing the divorce intention could be questioned, his reasons examined, and his petition denied. If the husband was found in the wrong, he could not be forced to go on living with the wife, but he was legally obliged to go on supporting her. Furthermore, women were also allowed to petition for divorce and to obtain legal support from the husband if their cause was just. They were also allowed to be represented in court by other women. So for the first time in history, women were, in effect, permitted to practice law.

He was himself a happily married man and the proud father of many children. He loved and respected the life of the family but knew it could not be manufactured or held together by law.

He expressed his feelings in this way:

Love is beautiful, and that a man and a woman loving each
other should live together is the will of God, but if there
comes a time when they cannot live in peace, let them part.
To have no relationship is not a disgrace; to have wrong
relations is, for disgrace means a lack of grace, discord—
and love is harmony.

Again the Emperor of ancient Rome was way ahead of
us. There is still a stigma to divorce and certainly to not
being married. Single and divorced people are regularly
discriminated against in many, many ways, legal and
social. What is perhaps worse, many people get married
and stay married more for the status and supposed security of marriage than for love. The number of divorces in
this country nowadays alarms many people. But what is
really cause for alarm is the much larger number of love-
less marriages that are endured in the name of respectability or out of the fear of the loss of security. These are
the relationships that lack real dignity. And these are the
relationships that subvert the integrity of the partners and
their unfortunate children. These relationships bring more
sorrow into our society than most people are willing to
admit.

Operating throughout the philosophy of Marcus Aurelius we find the idea that both God and humanity are
greater than we allow them to be with all our rigid theology, superstitious ritual, and reliance on a government
organism to regulate the lives of people. In his view, progress towards civilization must involve the gradual freedom of the individual from law and custom, with each
person more and more self-governing.

Marcus Aurelius was Emperor of Rome for nineteen
years. He died at age fifty-nine. Two years before his

death, while leading his army against a barbarian uprising in Asia, he found time to write his immortal *Meditations*. He was away from all his books and all his obligations to address the problems of others. In the midst of combat, in this foreign place, he found himself alone with his own thoughts. He put them down for himself, and they have survived as a blessing to us. These are the thoughts of a great mind given to a lifetime of great thought. The *Meditations* of Marcus Aurelius have been compared in quality to the gospels of the New Testament. They teach the same lesson: it is a lesson of the greatness of God operating through the consciousness of the elevated mind.

Men seek retreats for themselves, houses in the country, seashores, and mountains: and thou, too, art wont to desire such things very much. But this is altogether a mark of the most common sort of men, for it is in their power, whenever thou shalt choose, to retire into thyself. For nowhere either with more quiet or more freedom from trouble does a man retire to than into his own soul, particularly when he has within himself such thoughts that by looking into them he is immediately in perfect tranquility, which is nothing else than the good ordering of the mind.

4

Mystical Monk

Meister Eckhart
(1260–1327)

THEY SAY that Rome wasn't built in a day. It wasn't
destroyed in a day either. It took several centuries of
misrule and failure to empower the mindless superstition
that corrupted the spiritual life of the empire, making it
more and more vulnerable to discontent and subversion
from within and defenseless against attack from without.

The fabled fall of Rome began with the loss of control
over its far-flung territories and became final in A.D. 546
when the city itself was overrun by barbarian hordes from
Northern Europe.

The early Christian church by this time was still small
but highly organized and very well disciplined. It was
therefore able to exert tremendous influence in an otherwise topsy-turvy world. By diligent effort approaching
fanaticism it was able to emerge as the dominant religion
in a world of religious confusion and controversy. It became looked to as the religious system that would succeed

in bringing spiritual harmony where all the old religions had failed.

Both the forces of the government and the military came to see it as an essential unifying factor and so put their power behind the church. Christianity replaced various forms of paganism and became the state religion. There were mass conversions to this new religion impelled by government edict backed up by military power. The church facilitated these conversions by artfully adopting into its theology many of the old pagan superstitions, rituals, and celebrations. Its objective was no longer to convert by inspiring people's souls. It was now content to convert by coercing their obedience and controlling their lives. This was done by making people's physical well-being entirely dependent upon their religious conformity. And so the religion of brotherly love had become the religion of strict fatherly discipline. It regarded people as naughty children needing to be brought into line, by force if necessary—and it often was—or by allowing people to bring along their toys—the pagan ideas and practices they were used to.

There are some who observe that the famous conversion of the pagan world to Christianity was actually the conversion of fundamental Christian ideals—that is, the teaching of Jesus—to paganism.

The period of European history between the fall of Rome in the fifth century and the mid-thirteenth century has come to be known as the Dark Ages. Eight hundred years of darkness. Darkness of the mind. In this period all dissenting thought—which means any idea that seemed not to readily support the increasingly rigid, fearful, and superstitious theology of the church—was severely oppressed. Independent thinkers were few and underground. The works of the greatest minds of Greece and Rome were destroyed wherever found, and their ideas declared heresy. The only earthly source of truth was the church. In this case the "church" meant whatever person or group wielded the greatest political influence in the church at the time. It was not always, and perhaps not usually, the Pope. The doctrine of papal infallibility actually did not come about until the middle of the nineteenth century, as yet another futile attempt to keep the human mind in bondage.

The essence of correct thought in the Dark Ages was of God as a disembodied entity living somewhere above the world, who gave directions to the human race through the rulers of the church who were located in Rome. To live in truth one only had to listen to what Rome said was so, profess to believe it, teach and practice it, and die for it if necessary. Individual reasoning was discouraged. It gave the devil, who lived somewhere below the earth, a chance to come into the world and corrupt the work of the church. When one became the instrument of the devil, the only redemption was the cleansing of the spirit by fire. That meant burning up the body so the spirit could float freely up to God.

The human mind can be controlled by fear, and appeased by comfortable superstition, but not forever, because mind must move forward if life is to go on. Eventually the need to think freely will overcome every kind of fear, and the hunger for rightness will explode even the most tantalizing superstition.

By the middle of the thirteenth century many people were daring to think freely and to speak freely. This was especially dangerous to the church because, with the invention of the printing press, these unorthodox ideas were appearing in print and finding wide circulation and an increasingly agreeable audience.

The Dark Ages were drawing to a close, and the church was outraged. Its response was to create the infamous Inquisition to deal with the heretics who seemed to be springing up all over, and the Inquisition went about its bloody business with great intensity and an unholy relish. Never tell a person committed to ignorance that he may be wrong—especially if ignorance is providing him social status, political power, and a good living.

Most of these daring new freethinkers were scholars and even churchmen. The devil had penetrated close to home. This was cause for the greatest alarm in the church, and these people were pursued by the Inquisition with special fury.

One such churchman-scholar was the German monk Meister Eckhart. He was a member of the highly respected Dominican order, and was more than a simple cloistered monk. He was a noted university teacher at Paris and Cologne and had received a doctorate from the Pope himself. He was also an influential leader of the Dominican order.

Beyond this, we know little of his personal life, but he leaves behind the profound impression of a man of absolute serenity of character and clarity of vision. He was also regarded as a true and simple mystic. A mystic is a person who sees beyond what the world says is so.

Meister Eckhart's inner vision let him see beyond all the convoluted and parochial theology of the church of his day. What he saw beyond it was the presence of God as a universal beingness rather than a disembodied entity in the sky.

He wrote that God is pure being, not a person ruling over us but a presence within us. Therefore, nothing outside ourselves is the medium through which we know God. That would, of course, include the church. "Why do you look without for that which is within you?" he asked.

The presence of God, and the power, is to be found by every person within his or her own soul. Therefore our attention should always be directed to inner thought, not outer voices. Within ourselves there is the intelligence that knows all and reveals all. Therefore within ourselves there is always a perfect peace and purity. He tells us, "The exterior of man may be undergoing trials, but the interior man is quite free." This internal freedom is the atmosphere through which all the wisdom and power of the universal God comes to us. And in this atmosphere we can know the truth which will set us free from the problems of the world. This leads us to conclude that wisdom cannot be laid upon us by an external agency, including the church, as a reward for obedience or adoration. Nor can this wisdom be denied us by any outside agency for any reason whatsoever. We must then believe in and follow only that which seems right to us at soul level. "How can any external revelation help me unless it is verified by internal experience?"

When we think at soul level—that is, when we look for our wisdom within ourselves—we activate what he called a spark which brings the light and power of the all-knowing God into action within us. Until we do that, we deprive ourselves of real understanding while God patiently awaits our awakening.

Meister Eckhart reminds us that we cannot have wisdom by appearing to have wisdom, or overcome the burden of our ignorance by hiding it from the world. "A stone beneath the surface of the ground is just as heavy as a visible one," he explains.

In order to relate to life from soul level one must begin by annihilating self-interest. This means, according to Eckhart, simply emptying oneself out; letting go of attachment or dependency upon the things of the world which are in and of themselves meaningless. They are the products of thought, not the producer of life. When one becomes a desert, a place where no things can take root, one will be empty of things, and so become full of God.

This kind of thinking, if taken seriously, will create individuals, a race of individuals in fact, who will soon discover that they have no need for the blessings of their priests or the rituals of their church. Nor will they find themselves obliged to support its ambitions or serve its purposes. On such people the future expansion of human life depends, but because of such people the political and economic supremacy of the church is in grave danger. This indeed had to be considered heresy.

His greatest heresy, however, was his claim that the concept of the begetting of the Son by the Father did not refer to an historical event that took place centuries before in Bethlehem with the birth of Jesus. It was a way of describing the creative process by which God is eternally entering the soul of every person and thus providing a way for all people to achieve the consciousness of the Christ. The Father, he said, was eternally begetting the only-begotten. This, of course, struck a heavy blow against the tendency to worship Jesus as God in order to achieve salvation. It instead suggests that we should find our salvation by letting God do through each one of us what was done through Jesus. In other words, we ought to stop worshipping Jesus, which he never asked us to do in the first place, and start following his example, which he constantly implored us to do.

In the last year of his life the widely loved sixty-seven-year-old mystical monk was summoned before the Inquisition. His trial proved, as such trials usually did, several points of heresy in his teaching. He did recant and so was permitted to die in peace instead of in flames. It was the choice of a wise man who knew very well that truth once spoken can never be destroyed, and a fiery death would add nothing to the stature of his philosophy. He did what he could to save the souls of his inquisitors by keeping them from the sin of murdering his body. He was, after all, sworn by his priesthood to save souls, not condemn them, so even at this time of great personal stress, he was a truer priest than any of his inquisitors.

5

Cosmic Observer

Giordano Bruno
(1548-1600)

H E GREW up answering to the name of Filippo in a small village in the Kingdom of Naples. It was apparent to all that the child was exceptionally bright and inquisitive and destined for the scholar's life. In sixteenth-century Italy that meant destined for holy orders, for the holy Catholic church was virtually the one and only institution for advanced education.

Like Meister Eckhart three centuries before him, young Filippo entered the respected and powerful Dominican order. His teachers were delighted with him. He loved his studies and learned quickly and well. He was given the monastic name Giordano after the river Jordan. This was a name reserved for the most promising students, perhaps symbolizing the purity and power attributed to that river among the pious and imaginative.

In the course of his studies his teachers' delight came

to be mixed with a degree of agitation. Young Giordano turned out to be one of those challenging students teachers find hard to control, because he was hard to keep up with and wanted to learn a great deal more than they were prepared to teach. His restless mind pushed him beyond learning what every young Dominican should know and would not permit him to accept dogmatic conclusions based only on faith in the wisdom of those who laid such things before him.

He was eager to examine ideas and concepts that had been dismissed out of hand as false and dangerous by the church. Such ideas did not threaten the integrity of his mind or soul, but seemed to stir his soul and heighten his learning powers. He was not looking for something new or different to believe, but he wanted to know what it was in these things that made some people believe in them and profess them even though it caused them to be labeled heretic and placed them in very real danger of their lives.

One of the great heresies of the day was Arianism. It was an early form of Unitarianism. It rejected the divinity of Jesus and the idea that God existed as three separate persons, a Father, a Son, and a Holy Ghost. He did not become an Arian but believed their point of view had merit and did not see that it in any way threatened the real meaning of the teachings of Jesus.

The church managed to stamp out Arianism by bringing its leaders and prominent followers to the flames while Giordano was still a young man. However, his defense of this heresy would come back to haunt him many years later when he himself was tried before the Holy Inquisition as a heretic.

Giordano was ordained a priest at age twenty-four, and

at that moment passed from under the protection of his teachers, who could no longer cover up or excuse the excesses of his bright young mind. Now he was fully responsible for his views and entirely vulnerable to charges of heresy.

The young priest was not an iconoclast. He loved his church deeply. He loved all its rituals and rites. However, he saw them not as magic but as symbolic. For instance, he questioned the idea that in the sacrament of Holy Eucharist the bread and wine actually turned into the flesh and blood of Jesus when the priest pronounced the words of consecration. He saw this sacrament as a lovely and meaningful symbol of the desire to be spiritually one with Jesus. Giordano went further. The Bible, he reasoned, certainly could not be a factual account of our spiritual origins. Surely its stories were too fantastic and contradictory for this to be so. The many miracles reported were certainly not acts of God in defiance of the natural order. Though very important, were they not really allegorical devices used to powerfully impress us with the importance of the moral lessons of the Bible? In fact, could not all so-called miracles be explained in terms of natural law once we became more aware of the marvels of nature?

Giordano Bruno was from the beginning destined for a perilous existence. He was born into an age of extreme intolerance and given a mind that would not be harnessed even by fear of destruction. It proved to be his undoing. But he was not undone before he made a lasting contribution to man's eternal search for truth that could never be undone.

By the sixteenth century, dissatisfaction with the stranglehold of the church on human thought was widespread.

So was dissatisfaction with the enormous political and economic power of the church, which gave it the power to make or break people, to give to its favored few a secure and prosperous life, and leave the rest of the world to struggle along, accept their lot, and hope for a better life hereafter. The church, of course, also claimed to control the gateway to the hereafter and to have the power to send one to glory or to the eternal flames.

The race was evolving in spite of itself, and more and more people found it impossible to tolerate this kind of oppression. The Protestant Reformation was in full flower. The Catholic church had not only lost the minds and hearts of many thousands but had earned their fanatical hatred. The church had also lost political power and economic support from the once all-Catholic Europe. Its response was traditional: it became more rigidly dogmatic in teaching and more cruel and indiscriminate in the use of its temporal power.

The Inquisition was more powerful, more widespread, and more reckless now than ever before. It could rarely reach the heretics of the Reformation, who lived for the most part beyond its grasp. So in its frenzy it took off after the people still within the church who could be found to harbor the slightest doubts about the church's theology in its narrowest construction. Witch hunting was the order of the day. Torture was the will of God for those labeled heretic. And burning alive was the prescribed means for destroying their sinful flesh and letting their thus purified spirits rise to heaven. The church, of course, confiscated for its own treasury whatever earthly goods or property the poor soul left behind.

One might wonder how all this cruelty could ever be

justified in the minds of people professing the love of God, since God's love is for all. There is an answer to this, of course. It is an absurd answer, but then it served an absurd purpose. It was all done in the name of love. The church loved these heretics so much it had to step in and drive their unforgivable sin from them in order to purify their souls and make them worthy of entrance into heaven. First they tortured as much sin out of them as they could. Then to get every last trace of sin out of them, they burned their bodies. Was not fire the great purifier according to holy scripture?

Happily, we do not torture and burn people for their beliefs or their way of life anymore. At least, not as a matter of policy and certainly not as a rule. Modern society simply will not condone such common cruelty. But we still are victims of the idea that we are free to persecute those who view life differently, if we can get away with it. Especially if we can convince ourselves that it is for their own good, that is, for love of God and humankind. This is the basis of the kill-for-Jesus mentality that lies just beneath the surface of so much of our fearful, fundamentalist fervor today. It pops up every once in a while with the bombing of an abortion clinic. It raised its ugly head recently when the minister of a large and narrow congregation in California exhorted his people to pray for the death of a certain Supreme Court Justice who was, in his opinion, handing down decisions not consistent with God's will.

The spiritual descendants of the pious and vicious Inquistors are among us today, but the law is not so totally on their side anymore. So they disguise their ill will towards poeple whose beliefs or way of life offend them by picketing their churches, schools, and activities, and shouting things like "We love you but we hate your sin."

As nonsensical as this is, it is better than throwing fire-bombs. However, it suggests that the willingness to oppress people because of their belief still outweighs the willingness to love them because of their being. Too many church people seem to find themselves opposed to their brethren, in denying them their rights to housing or employment or full protection of the law. If we really love people, the power of love will entirely obliterate our fear and loathing of their "sin." That's what real love really does—it casts out fear. The instant we do harm of any kind to another, for any reason, we have abandoned love altogether.

Following his ordination, Giordano's persistence in exploring forbidden territory made him more and more of a liability to the Dominican order. Two years after his ordination the order started proceedings to discipline or perhaps even expel him. Imprisonment was a distinct possibility. In fear of this he left the order and spent the next sixteen years wandering through Europe, taking refuge wherever he could for as long as he could, always staying just a few paces ahead of the Holy Inquisition. He was, in time, excommunicated by the church and so became even more vulnerable to arrest, torture, and death.

He was safe nowhere in Europe, which meant nowhere in the civilized world, not even in the rapidly multiplying Protestant strongholds of Northern Europe, because his ideas, so eloquently expressed in his teaching and his writing, went much further beyond orthodoxy than even the Protestant reformers were willing to tread.

As the years went by and Giordano travelled on alone,

free from the discipline of monastic life and no longer having to answer to superiors for his views, his mind grew more fertile, his interests broadened, and he quite unintentionally descended deeper and deeper into heresy.

He was strongly attracted to the new science of astronomy and was much taken with the ideas of Copernicus, who had died shortly before Giordano's birth. Copernicus had been forced by the Inquisition to recant his astronomical theories before his death. But, of course, his writings were still secretly circulated, and Giordano, always receptive to forbidden knowledge, quite naturally came upon them.

Copernicus theorized that the sun did not revolve around the earth but that the earth and its sister planets revolved around the sun. Science, of course, would prove this theory correct. But in the sixteenth century there was no way to prove it scientifically. And if there had been, neither the Catholic nor Protestant dogmatic theologians of the day would have listened.

It was rank heresy, totally inconsistent with Christian doctrine on all sides. The universe, by orthodox reasoning, had to be earth-centered, with sun and moon and stars and everything in the universe created specifically to serve life on earth. The account of the Creation in the book of Genesis made this perfectly clear. Furthermore, was not the earth the place where God placed his ultimate creation, humankind? And was it not to this place God sent his only Son, Jesus, to suffer and die for our sins? And—in the Catholic view at least—did not the Son of God himself establish the Holy Church and the succession of the Papacy to continue to save us from sin and to regulate the affairs of the universe? The Copernican theory was surely a subversive theory sent by the devil himself to erode the authority of the Holy Church and to lure us into a sense of meaninglessness and degradation.

These outraged arguments made slight impression on Giordano. His only response was to take the ideas of Copernicus a giant step forward. He speculated that if the earth and all her sister planets revolved around the sun, then it was reasonable to assume that the most distant stars were other earths and had other planets and revolved around other suns of their own. Perhaps, then, this was a clue that the universe extended to infinity and was governed by an Infinite Deity, a Supreme Creative Intelligence that was much more vast in scope and purpose than the God of the mighty theologians.

As well as being infinite, such a Deity must also be eternal. As such, Its existence and Its harmony must operate undisturbed by our wickedness and uninfluenced by our piety. It must be an impersonal force or intelligence operating entirely independently of us—giving us its power, but not being affected by our use or misuse of that power.

There is, following this line of reasoning, no divine retribution for sin, no divine blessing for virtue, and no person or institution divinely appointed to speak for the Deity or act in any way with divine authority. Any authority we have, we have by virtue of our understanding of the nature of things, and our individual commitment to bring ourselves into harmony with natural law. We do not improve our understanding or find harmony by accepting the ideas of others out of faith or fear. We grow and find peace only by training our minds to look at life objectively, accepting nothing as true until we can prove its worth in our lives.

This, of course, is the soul of scientific thought and the anathema of religious superstition.

Having stripped all earthly religion of any claim to divine authority, Giordano went on to suggest the proper source of all earthly authority. Moral conduct, he proposed, is natural to humankind. It does not have to be imposed upon us and cannot be imported by the courting or worship of any supernatural power. Goodness is a natural impulse in the soul which will grow and flourish in the arena of free personal expression. All power on earth should properly be directed to protecting, defending, and encouraging every individual to fully experience life in his or her own way and thus release in the world the goodness of the soul.

There is in this philosophy no place for sword or cross; no place of any kind for any tyranny, religious or temporal; no place for dogma and sectarianism, and no excuse for torture and murder, not even in the name of love or for the glory of God.

There was, in the sixteenth-century world, no place for Giordano Bruno. His ideas would surely tear the world, as it then existed, apart.

The Holy Inquisition at last caught up with him. Even recanting could not have saved him from torture or the flames. The fact that he had many defenders even within the church did not save him. It only delayed the inevitable and added years to his misery. He was held for eight years in the dungeons of the Inquisition at Rome.

His misery came to an end on February 17, 1600. Rome was decked out for the celebration of a Jubilee year in the life of the Holy Church. Pious pilgrims flocked from all over Catholic Europe. The humble came to repent. The crippled came there to be healed. Cardinals, kings, and princes came to be praised. Merchants came to sell their wares. Gamblers, whores, and con men of every kind came to ply their trades.

All came to witness the kick-off of the Jubilee year—the burning of the arch-heretic, Giordano Bruno.

At dawn the tortured and broken body of the fifty-two-year-old man was dragged up from the dungeon and paraded through the streets to the Campo dei Fiori. There, before a record crowd of the faithful, he was stripped and tied to a stake. He tried to speak, but his words were words of contempt and so he was gagged. His tormentors held an image of Jesus up to him, but he averted his eyes. The crowd jeered furiously at the gall of this terrible sinner. The fire was lit and to the immense delight of the cheering crowd this tool of the devil was burned alive.

As the smoke from the stake rose up to the sky, the church bells of Rome pealed, celebrating the deliverance of one more purified soul into the bosom of God.

6

God-Intoxicated Man of Amsterdam

Benedict de Spinoza
(1632–1677)

LIFE IS growth. In the case of human life we grow, expand, and prosper when we are thinking correctly and so are living in a consciousness that is established in right ideas. People have always been searching for the truth, or that which is right. So eager are we to be right that we are willing to discover truth at any cost. Unfortunately, we forget that the cost of knowing the truth cannot be levied on other people, but must be charged against our own account.

There is really only one way to prove that your opinion is a good and true opinion. That is by living, by making it the standard in all your personal activity, by letting it guide the way you think in the privacy of your mind and the way you conduct yourself in all your dealings with the world at large.

If what we hold to be true is indeed true, it will bring us peace of mind and success in all our affairs. If we do not have inner peace or if we are too much upset by the world around us, the problem lies within ourselves, in the area of our belief, in the way we think and the attitudes we live with.

The person who is too much impelled to getting other people to conform to his opinions or to live by his standards is not being well served by his own opinions or his own standards. There is something wrong with them and so there is something wrong with him. He is in pain. He is not enjoying life. And somehow he thinks that his pain will be all right if he can get other people to share it, by thinking like him and living by his standards. Misery really does love company. If other people will not share in the company of his consciousness, he is terribly offended and can become quite cruel.

There is a right way for each of us to think and to conduct our lives. And each of us can find it if we will pay the price instead of trying to pass the price on to others. The price of right ideas is the surrender of wrong ones. And the person who will find peace and right direction is the person who is committed to the business of reviewing his or her own thought objectively, always willing to consider new ideas and, if necessary, abandon old ones. In order to be this kind of person we must get over the habit of justifying our ideas by getting other people to agree with them, and scorning, criticizing, or actually punishing people who do not.

People point with alarm to all the dreadful problems of the world and say, "Don't I have an obligation to do something about this?" I think we all have an obligation to the world. But surely it can't be to bring more suffering and cruelty into it. Our obligation to the world is not to solve all of its problems, but to refuse to be one of them. It is to present the world with one honest mind, one loving heart, and one more productive life. This is our obligation. If seriously accepted, it will take as much time and energy as we are able to give it. The person who is really committed to making such a contribution will have very little time or energy to be bothered much about what other people are doing. And yet such a person will be a dynamic influence for good by virtue of what he or she is and is becoming. And he or she will be living life correctly. Spinoza put it this way: "To be what we are, to become what we are capable of becoming, is the only aim of life."

The only thing we really have to offer each other is inspiration. We cannot give people anything. We can only awaken them to something within themselves, and this is not done with argument, but by example. John Wesley said, "No man is worthy to be called a teacher unless he is a teacher of teachers." A great artist is one who inspires other artists. A great writer is one who inspires other writers. In other words, we do great work when we inspire others to do likewise, not when we merely please, amuse, distract, or tantalize them, but when, by virtue of what we are and what we do, we inspire them into positive, productive activity of their own.

This is the lasting genius of Spinoza. He is the philosopher's philosopher. His greatness comes not merely from the fine sentiments expressed in his writings, but from the way he put his ideas into action in his life, at a time and in a place that made it particularly hard to do so.

Spinoza tells us, "A singular strength of mind is required to enable a man to live among others constantly with his own ideas and convictions, to be master of himself, and not fall into habits or exhibit the same passions as those with whom he associates."

He is called the God-Intoxicated Man of Amsterdam because in the midst of life-long disapproval from all sides, he lived in a consciousness of personal exultation. Having discovered that God is all there really is, and that God lived and moved for him only within his own consciousness, he was able to ignore the threatening clamor all around him. He was able to go his way and do his thing without fear for himself or hatred for his tormentors. And so he lived in peace and produced a body of work that has inspired the greatest minds down through the years.

He was born Baruch Spinoza, a Jew of Spanish and Portuguese extraction. His family had fled Spain during the reign of Ferdinand and Isabella. These Most Catholic Majesties had given their large and prosperous population of Jewish subjects the option to convert to Catholicism or get out. They were given thirty days to decide. Many converted. But many others, who loved their own faith, departed looking for a more tolerant environment. Spinoza's forebears—and many other Iberian Jews—were on the move for many years and eventually settled in Amsterdam after Holland had become Protestant. Legally, they were safe there. Socially, they were despised. The Jewish community responded by living totally apart both physically and socially. They formed their own exclusive community in their own part of the city and did not welcome non-Jews onto their turf or into their society. In other words, they created a ghetto. In time they found, as others were not welcome to come into their ghetto, they were not welcome to leave it. And they responded to this physical confinement by becoming more and more traditional in their thinking and intolerant and contemptuous of all thought that did not line up with the most narrow interpretations of their traditions.

The Jews of Amsterdam developed an excellent system of education for their youth, and young Baruch was a fine student in both religious and secular studies. He was also quick to learn his father's trade—that of lens-grinder. He was to support himself throughout his life in that occupation. He believed that in order to think freely one must be able to support himself independently, and he insisted that every man should have a trade and earn his living with his hands, because when the hands are busy and productive, then the mind is free.

While still in his teens, Baruch became impressed with a small Protestant sect that had come from Germany to Holland to escape religious persecution. This sect was founded by Menno Simons and was called Mennonite. The Mennonites had swung much further away from Catholicism than Luther had. They rejected a paid priesthood as well as an oath of allegiance to any creed. "A priest," said Menno, "is a man who thrives on sacred relations between man and God, and is little better than a person who would live on the love-emotions of men and women." He said that men could go to God without either priest or church, and pray in secret. The Mennonites believed in hard work and simple living. They refused to take oaths, to hold civil office, and to go to war.

In Holland, like the Jews, the Mennonites were legally

protected but socially despised. Unlike the Jews, they did not respond by becoming bitter and theocratic. Their response was one of relief and quiet dedication to their way of plain and peaceful living.

Young Spinoza learned from these simple and earnest people that a person's life was not shaped by his theological devotion, but by his personal belief. The Mennonites confessed that they knew nothing but hoped for much. The learned rabbis the boy had encountered claimed to know everything but hoped for little. Baruch's affection for these outsiders, these infidels, reached the ears of the rabbis. He was summoned to the synagogue to defend himself. His judges were furious. He was calm. To their horror, he expressed the belief that God might possibly have revealed Himself to other people besides the Jews:

> "Then you are not a Jew!" was the answer.
> "Yes, I am a Jew, and I love my faith."
> "But is it not all to you?"
> "I confess that occasionally I have found what seems to be truth outside of the law."

That did it! He was thrown out of the synagogue and out of the ghetto. His own brothers and sisters refused him shelter. So did his father. So did all the others. The curse of Israel was upon him.

Here, in part, is the document that severed him forever from his Jewish roots:

> *The Lord blot out his name under heaven. The Lord set him apart for destruction, with all the curses of the firmament that are written in the Book of Law. There shall be no one speak to him, no man write to him, no man show him any kindness, no man stay under the same roof with him, no man come nigh him.*

At the age of twenty, Spinoza found refuge among the Mennonites and his life began.

In later years, long after Baruch Spinoza had vanished and Benedict Spinoza had appeared, he looked back upon all this and all the rest of his long experience as one man searching for one God and told us this:

Men are so made as to resent nothing more impatiently than to be treated as criminal on account of opinions which they deem to be true, and charged as guilty for simply what wakes their affection to God and men. Hence laws about opinions are aimed not at the base but at the noble, and tend not to restrain the evil-minded but rather to irritate the good, and cannot be enforced without great peril to government.

What evil can be imagined greater for a State, than that honorable men, because they have thoughts of their own and cannot act a lie, are sent as culprits into exile!

What more baneful thing than that men, for no guilt or wrongdoing, but for the general largeness of their minds, should be taken for enemies and led off to death, and that the torture-bed, the terror of the bad, should become, to the shame of authority, the finest stage for the public spectacle of endurance and virtue.

Spinoza lived his life alone. It was not a long life but a full one and the one he chose as necessary to his character. He was surrounded on all sides by those who despised him—the stern Dutch Protestants for being a Jew, the Jews for being an infidel. The small and equally shunned Mennonite community continued to look on him with favor, but its friendship for him merely aggravated the enmity surrounding him. There were infidels among the Dutch who perceived the excellence of his character and showed him kindness as they could. But none of them were able to win for him the approbation of the majority.

His real security was in his own consciousness and the laws of the land which forbade legalized persecution on theological grounds. It is interesting how the courage of would-be religious persecutors is dampened when active persecution is not legalized. That is, when they themselves stand to suffer for the crimes they would gladly commit in the name of God.

Spinoza found peace in the midst of all this because he looked for peace in the right place, within his own consciousness. And he practiced peace by developing his own understanding. He did not respond to the hostility of others in kind, not in his actions and, more importantly, not in his own heart. He tells us about it in this statement: "I saw that all things which occasioned me any anxiety had in themselves nothing of good or evil except insofar as my mind was moved by them." In the same vein he wrote, "It follows absolutely that one who uses his understanding correctly can fall prey to no sorrow."

So Spinoza kept to himself, living always in plain accommodations provided by kindly persons who did not understand him but believed in him, being touched by his simple goodness. He earned a small living as a lens-grinder, working at this only as much as necessary to see to his basic needs. Most of his time and energy was devoted to working out his philosophy and writing it down. His writings were circulated throughout Europe and had a tremendous influence in intellectual circles. Great people came from all over to see him and discuss ideas. Some of them offered him financial support so he could devote full time to his thinking and writing. He gently refused such offers. He believed that if he were financially free from earning a living from his trade, the quality of his thought might suffer. "You cannot think intensely and intently all of the time," he said. "Those who try it are never able to dive deep or soar high. Man should work and busy himself with the commonplace, rest himself for his flight, and when the moment of transfiguration comes, make the best of it."

Spinoza's philosophy is based upon a concept of God as an infinite beingness which is both the source and substance of all life, that which does all the creating and fills all creation. This infinite being exists necessarily, that is, because it must. Its existence is not because of anything, yet its creative nature is the cause of all things.

Why we exist is not knowable. But since that which created us represents total intelligence, we must assume there is a good reason for our existence. Since we can think before we can do anything else, thought must be our primary function and the key to our unfoldment. The nature and quality of our thought, then, is what determines the nature and quality of the conditions our thought creates.

We can improve the nature and quality of our thought only by a personal inquiry into our thinking, that is, only by thinking about our thinking. We will thus come to recognize the kinds of ideas or attitudes that produce a good effect when we apply them to the conduct of our lives.

So the primary activity of life is the activity of mind seeking wisdom, which is mind inquiring into the nature of God. This must also be the primary purpose of religion, because religion is nothing more than a human invention. Its purpose is to help us improve the quality of our individual lives and thus of life in the world. Its purpose is not to prepare us through pain and sorrow and hardship for a better life beyond this world.

We carry within our being an essential desire to know better in order to live better. It can never be satisfied by explanations that make no sense to us and it can never be stifled by coercion or fear of coercion, at least not indefinitely. This desire is also our essential virtue, and only through its pursuit do we come into the understanding that will let us overcome the problems of our environment.

When we are following this desire and practicing this virtue, we find happiness. When we are not, we are immersed in sadness. All our emotional states are built upon happiness or sadness, that is, desire fulfilled or desire thwarted. Love is happiness tied to the idea of an external cause. We hate what we think brings us sadness. Hope is the expectation of future happiness. Fear is the expectation of future sadness. We can be hopeful only if we realize that we are permanently connected to God and that infinite goodness is always at hand. If we think our good comes from a concept of a withholding God or from any earthly source whose givingness is not entirely dependable, we are fearful. The mind immersed in fear creates pain and limitation in the life of the individual and contributes negatively to the life of the world.

So the conditions of our life, by Spinoza's reckoning, spring forth identically from the condition of our consciousness. Thoughts create things and are really the mental equivalents of the things they create. For every physical event there is a parallel or corresponding mental event. But mind is the originator and, therefore, life must be reordered by the reordering of thought.

Both church and government, in Spinoza's view, in order to have a legitimate reason for existence, must serve the individual. They must be so constructed as to encourage, promote, and reward free thinking and independent living. If either fails to do this, it betrays its purpose and no person is under obligation to support it, honor it, or obey it. This does not mean that we should become embroiled in contention with an oppressive religious or governmental institution. It is not a call to terrorism or armed revolt or any other kind of violent activity. It is, rather, a challenge to think your own thoughts, go your own way, and do your own thing in the face of praise or in the face of condemnation. That is, to have the courage and honesty to pay the price for your own convictions.

Spinoza paid the price and found it not to be too high once he realized that the real source of his good was within himself. He lived in peace and serenity in the midst of unending outrage, perfectly secure as in the eye of a hurricane. He died without illness or suffering at age forty-three. According to one biographer, "His passing was like a sigh." One fine day he simply drifted away while alone and at his work.

7

Mystical Scientist

Emanuel Swedenborg
(1688–1772)

WHO KNOWS where originality ends and insanity begins? The world has always counted as sane only people whose ideas are obvious. Every original idea has at its emergence been considered madness, or at least very peculiar. And the individual who persists in espousing original ideas—ideas not immediately recognizable as valid or not provable using current standards of evidence —is also viewed as weird and unstable, a person to be avoided.

Yet original ideas are what make civilization move forward. We do not progress by devotion to the obvious, but only through exploration of the new, the unproven, and the tantalizing.

Frequently a new idea presents itself long before it can be cleverly and logically explained. Such ideas race like meteors through the minds of persons who have dedicated themselves to knowing more, to understanding better, and to seeing more deeply into the infinite nature of things. The word *mystic* is sometimes used to describe people who perceive more than they can sensibly explain or prove. Sometimes we revere such people, sometimes we mock them. But they are always held at arm's length, deprived of the human warmth that is as important to their stability as it is to anyone else's. Perhaps that is why so many people who have deeper insights choose to dismiss them or at least keep them to themselves. Few people have the spiritual confidence to expose their most speculative thoughts to the world and still find in life the harmony and acceptance that we all crave.

Emanuel Swedenborg was one of those few. The published works through which the world knows him were done late in his life. His reputation as a thorough-going, hard-headed scientist was well established in his own country and elsewhere in Europe. He was a man of wealth and influence, well loved by all who knew him.

At age fifty-six he reported having an unworldly experience. He was flooded by a great light which engulfed his entire being. He lost consciousness for a moment and was then reawakened by a beautiful and reassuring voice. It was, he said, the voice of Christ. It told him that he would come to see the deepest truths of the world of spirit and directed him to write about these truths for the benefit of all humanity. He devoted the rest of his long life to doing that. From what he revealed in the written works that followed this event, we draw a major contribution to the spiritual sanity of the world.

This is not to say that every word Swedenborg wrote was a precious pearl of truth, or that every concept he advanced was a world-shattering concept. The truth is that much of his writing makes no sense at all. It is obviously the recording of ideas that defy even our most honest and passionate desire to find understanding. But enough of it does make supreme good sense to justify the lasting fame of this strange and brilliant man.

Swedenborg's later works are an embarrassment to scholars dedicated to a purely intellectual approach to greater understanding. This is because of the claimed source of his literary output. It's just too spooky to be quite respectable. But embarrassed or not, no devoted scholar can resist studying Swedenborg, because what is to be found in the best of his thinking is well worth discovering.

In our own time Einstein developed his remarkable theories by applying his powers of deduction to observed phenomena and drawing from within his own mind theories that were not explainable in terms of classical physics. Yet these theories have caused us to reshape our ideas of time and space and so have unlocked a whole new world of possibility. Had Einstein perceived his theories as having been delivered to his contemplating mind by disembodied entities of the spirit world, we would not have listened to him. We may even have locked him up. As it happened, we accepted his incomprehensible speculations as coming from the mind of a genius. We have eagerly and profitably pursued them.

Both Einstein and Swedenborg were highly disciplined minds operating upon a vast amount of accumulated information and resorting to the power of imagination to take them beyond the limitations of logical explanation.

Both of these men were thus able to postulate new theories which were baffling to more earthbound thinkers at first but quite productive as they were explored. Both of them also came up with output that is still incomprehensible to the rest of us and has never been explainable by themselves. Some of it is quite possibly nonsense.

But we dismiss Einstein's nonsense, because we view him as a scientific genius. With Einstein we are willing to take the best and forgive the rest. However, in Swedenborg's case, we discount his entire body of work, pointing to his nonsense as our reason. What really turns us off is the manner in which his ideas came to him. We don't want to be made the fool by clinging to the words of someone who claims to see and hear things. On the other hand, Swedenborg has always been the darling of those people who equate genius with simple confusion. There are people who do not feel that art is great art unless it defies interpretation, or that music is great unless it offends our sense of harmony, or that a teacher is truly wise if he is in the habit of making himself perfectly clear. These dear people are not happy with any authority that does not confound them, because they really do not want to understand. They want to believe that great understanding is always just beyond them. They want to be credited for reaching out and then be set free to go on and believe whatever suits their particular purposes or fits within the limitations of their intellect.

Such people have made Swedenborg a saint and his writings holy writ. They refer to him with great reverence and quote his writings with dour authority, putting whatever meaning on them that is consistent with their prejudice. A church was organized in Swedenborg's name during his own lifetime by such devotees. It still exists and is as lacking in his depth and generosity of spirit as the orthodox Christian churches are lacking in the spirit of Jesus.

A look at his origins and early life provides important insight into the nature of this brilliant and complex man.

He was born in Stockholm. At the end of the seventeenth century Sweden and all of Scandinavia were thoroughly Protestant—Lutheran, to be precise. Lutheranism was the state religion in Sweden. Its place and religious authority were secured by both government edict and the will of the vast majority of the population. There was little passion for uncovering religious dissent—unless it be Roman Catholic, of course. The Lutheran church was morally rigid, but not intolerant of intellectual speculation and not threatened by any ideas that did not openly confront its moral authority or political exclusivity.

Emanuel's father was a Lutheran bishop and a professor of theology. He was also a spiritualist. He claimed to hear voices from the spirit world and to thus receive deeply meaningful spiritual instruction. We may safely assume that this instruction was supportive of his Lutheran theology. Otherwise, he would have been in serious trouble.

His young son adored him and the affection was abundantly returned. Father and son spent much time together. They regularly went mountain climbing and fishing in the beautiful fjords. Modern child psychologists would heartily applaud this ideal man-to-man, father-son relationship. They would have no difficulty in explaining why, at the age of seven, little Emanuel claimed to hear spirit voices just like Papa. Not only did he hear these voices, he saw angels flying about.

This may have pleased Papa, but it definitely did not please Mama, who had already had enough of Papa's otherworldliness. The good woman put her foot down. She insisted that the bishop keep his spiritual voices to himself while she addressed herself to seeing that the boy became fully involved in a course of practical and reasonable education. And so he did.

Emanuel proved an exceptionally gifted student and developed expertise in all subjects, particularly science, mathematics, and languages. He moved fast and at twenty-one received his Ph.D. His scholarship brought him to the attention and under the patronage of the King of Sweden. He seemed destined for a career in the diplomatic service, and as part of his grooming for this he was sent by the government on a grand tour of the great capitals of Europe. In each city he spent his time searching out the great men of the day who knew the most about mathematics, geology, anatomy, physics, and other scientific disciplines. He used his consular credentials to get interviews with them, and so his education continued.

On his return to Sweden he was employed by the government as a scientific advisor, bringing his expertise to various government projects. His service was spectacular, earning him rapid promotion and excellent income. At one point he was called upon to break a blockade by transferring ships overland a distance of fourteen miles. He did this by inventing and constructing a roller railway. For this he was knighted by the king.

In the course of his government service he conceived the possibility of a boat that would sail under the sea, a gun that would fire a thousand bullets in a minute, a flying machine, and a mechanical chariot that would go twenty miles an hour. All this in the early eighteenth century and all too advanced to be considered anything more than fanciful speculation. Everyone knew these things could never be.

One idea that he did pursue and work out in detail was a plan of mathematics that became our present decimal system.

By middle age Swedenborg had it all—everything the average person dreams of but never gets. He was rich, a proven genius, honored and beloved by all from king to ordinary citizen. He was also handsome and robustly healthy. He had it all and thought he had seen it all. At age forty-six he wrote a book on science which he intended to be his last great contribution. "As this is probably the last book I shall ever write," said he, "I desire here to make known to posterity these thoughts which so far as I know have never been explained before."

This book, *The Principles of Natural Things,* is a lengthy and difficult exposition of theories of light, atomism, crystallography, the physiology of the human brain, and the origin of the species and of the universe. The language of the book is colorful, the arguments dazzling, and the display of imagination thought-provoking in the extreme. It is not light reading. But it has been avidly read by all the great scientific thinkers since that time, and most of the theories so fancifully advanced in it have come to be accepted as scientific fact.

As it happens this book was by no means Swedenborg's last, nor did it mark the end of his career. It marked the end of the first glorious phase of his life and the beginning of the second, which was to end with his death thirty-eight years later at the age of eighty-four.

In 1745 following his great spiritual experience, he published a very different kind of book, *On the Love and Wisdom of God.* It is primarily this text, and his final book, *The True Christian Religion,* published in 1771, that gives us the Swedenborgian spiritual philosophy with all its sense and nonsense.

There is, according to Swedenborg, a natural harmony between body and soul, between our outer being and our inner being. The "fall of Man" was not an historical event, but was a point in our evolution where we, as a race, experienced a separation of soul from body, so that the infinite knowledge of the soul is locked into our being, but not available to us through the operation of our logical mind. In order to know more, we must first use what we already logically know to create a moral and ethical life for ourselves and so free our minds and hearts from error. Having accomplished this, we must then reach within for our greater understanding.

He says, "There has been given to man the ability to elevate his understanding into the light in which the angels are, that he may see what he must will and what he must do."

It seems, then, that we do have the capacity to overcome the fears and limitations of the world. And that this is done first by making peace with ourselves in the world and then looking beyond the ideas of the world for our salvation.

Swedenborg calls this being regenerated. With our regeneration comes freedom from all the things that threaten to defeat us. "An unregenerated man," he wrote, "is like one who sees phantoms at night, and afterwards, when he is being regenerated, he is the same man seeing in the early dawn that the things he saw at night are delusions." So, in this process of regeneration, nothing really changes but our perception of things. A change of mind is sufficient to set us free.

If it is that simple, we may ask why so many people don't do it. As if anticipating this question, Swedenborg explains:

> *Man does not wish to come out of spiritual servitude into spiritual liberty, for the reason, first, that he does not know what spiritual servitude is, and what spiritual liberty is; he does not possess the truths that teach this, and without truths spiritual servitude is believed to be freedom, and spiritual freedom to be servitude.*

He seems to be describing what spiritual leaders have more recently described as "living upside-down." The world encourages us to believe that our troubles are caused by what other people are doing or by what has been done in the past. Therefore, to get out of trouble, we spend a good deal of energy trying to change other people and wipe out the past. In doing so we place ourselves in spiritual servitude. All our energy is spent on the impossible. Spiritual liberty lies beyond other people and the past and the world of "fact" altogether. But we view any kind of personal spiritual development as a chore, a burden, something we can't spare the time for. This attitude, if not caused by, is certainly reinforced by the morbidity and hopelessness of the kind of religions that the world so piously dishes up for us. So we tend not to bother with our own spiritual development too much, because we see it as servitude rather than the way to freedom.

Central to Swedenborg's revealed spiritual wisdom is

the theory that there is a correspondence between the spiritual and the physical. Every person lives on both levels at once. What is experienced within has a direct effect on what is experienced without. What is experienced without—that is, what we allow ourselves to think, say, and do—has a direct effect on the condition of our inner being—our soul. We purify our soul by selecting better ideas to live with, expressing ourselves in nobler terms, and engaging ourselves in healthy pursuits. The soul responds by creating an inner peace and clarity that makes it easier to view life correctly and live life prosperously.

The right ordering of our soul-body relationship, following Swedenborg's theories, brings us into a "mystical communion" with God, the source of all goodness.

Emanuel Swedenborg lived a long, healthy and prosperous life by becoming an example of the spiritual philosophy he so clearly and ardently articulated. So perhaps practicing what one preaches not only proves the validity of what is being preached, but also improves the vitality of the preacher.

Wouldn't it be interesting if public opinion demanded that all who preached goodness be required to prove their goodness? That all who claimed to have a way be obliged to show how they were taking that way and where it had brought them from and where it had brought them to? It would be so refreshing if our leaders, especially our "spiritual" leaders, would set us a clear example before they loaded upon us a lofty challenge. This might well be the kind of thing that really would save the world.

8

Apostle of Reason

Voltaire
(1694–1778)

H E WAS born François-Marie Arouet, but he abandoned that name at age twenty-one when it became
clear that his father, who gave him the name to begin
with, had abandoned him. The old man had not turned
his back on his son lightly, for he was not a cruel man,
merely a fearful one. He had already gone out on a very
shaky limb to protect the boy's life and preserve his freedom. He found decent employment for him at the royal
court in Holland after the publication of one of his first
little essays, an outrageously witty exposé of the doings
of certain persons at the French court. The essay was published anonymously, but the elder Arouet recognized the
very distinct style and knew it was only a matter of time
before serious trouble was upon them all. The Bastille
awaited with pleasure writers of such cheek.

His sojourn in Holland was to be the first of many

exiles, enforced and self-imposed, in a long and turbulent life. He soon disturbed the sensitivity of the Dutch court by becoming romantically involved with a prominent and married noblewoman, and with the the lady's daughter as well. The ensuing scandal brought his exile to an end, and François was shipped back to Paris.

Before long his writing got him into further trouble. He published a poem making a great fool out of both the Regent of France and his beloved daughter, the Duchess de Berri. Once gain he escaped the Bastille through the intervention of his frantic father. This time he was legally exiled to a point three hundred miles beyond Paris and forbidden to come one step nearer on threat of imprisonment or worse.

This exile was brief and was brought to an end by the same talent that created it. The boy wrote a dazzling poem for the regent in which he managed to eloquently protest his innocence and his undying devotion to the great man whom he claimed to regard as an absolute paragon of virtue. Fortunately the "great man" was both mild-tempered and vain, and so a pardon was granted.

On the boy's return to Paris, his father refused to allow him to live at home. He knew better than anyone at this time that the trouble was not over, but was just beginning. So François was on his own, living in boardinghouses and making some kind of living by writing plays, acting in them, and applying himself to developing the literary skills which, wedded to his natural wit and talent for ridicule, would turn him into France's greatest essayist, playwright, and social critic.

But before he would gain that distinction, he would live

through a lot of troubles, most of them caused by the tireless output of his lethal pen. By the time he was twenty-one the father's greatest fear was visited upon the son. François was in jail, the Bastille, serving a year's sentence on a charge of expressing in print his congratulations to the people of France on the death of Louis XIV. Not only was he locked up, but he was not allowed pens or paper because of his history of abuse of these good things. He was allowed books of his choice, however, and spent the time in prison reading the classics and perfecting his Latin and Greek. In time, he was allowed to organize theatrical performances within the prison and at last permitted pen and paper on the promise that he would use them only to translate the Bible.

His time in the Bastille did not make a new man of him, but a better man, a man who knew how both to survive and to thrive while doing what his own nature best fitted him to do. While in prison he changed his name. He abandoned François-Marie Arouet, not in anger towards his father, but to signal to himself and the world that he was in every way on his own. He chose the name Voltaire, a word of his own coining. No one else had ever been called by this name, and no one else ever would be.

Eighteenth-century France was a bastion of political and religious autocracy. King and church still reigned supreme, but both were badly shaken by the threat of new political ideas and by the heresy of the Protestant Reformation. England had already executed an anointed and reigning monarch and now was governed by kings whose power was being systematically eroded by a parliamentary government that was more and more in the hands of the middle class. Most of northern Europe was steeped in Protestant heresy, and the holy Catholic church was actually outlawed.

France responded to this outrage by clamping down severely on every kind of political and religious dissent. Recognizing that trouble begins with new ideas, the government became the implacable enemy of any person or group who expressed any ideas not consistent with what was easily recognizable as supporting the supreme authority of king and church in their unholy alliance to control the lives, command the obedience, and feed upon the labors of all people.

Both king and church regarded God as the source of their omnipotence. Anyone who seemed to threaten it was deemed ungodly and therefore entirely disposable, like so much devilish filth to be washed off the face of the earth. Winning the hearts and minds of people was not their objective. They felt that those belonged to them by the will of God. What they were after was their obedience, their servility, and their money.

Witch-hunts were the order of the day. Imprisonment without evidence and without trial was commonplace. Torture was still viewed as the God-ordained way to purge the "sinners" of their "sins" and to make such "sins" extremely unattractive to others.

Public execution was just and considered good for the public morale. Death by the axe was the most merciful method. Burning at the stake was still in vogue. Being pulled apart by horses made to run in different directions was not uncommon and was always a crowd-pleaser. Following the death of the devilish dissenter, his property was confiscated to be added to the bulging fortunes of either king or church. Innocent heirs were left penniless to join the swelling ranks of the dirt poor.

We sometimes look back with outrage on the bloody excesses of the French Revolution that eventually toppled this wicked system. It is good to remember that the revolutionaries developed their taste for mindless cruelty at the feet of their masters.

This great revolution did not come until Voltaire was safely in his grave. During his lifetime the possibility of such a sudden and total upheaval was more than even he ever dreamed of, and it's just as well that he didn't have to live through it. Although his ideas certainly were a major influence leading to the revolution, his absolute independence of mind and intolerance of intolerance would surely have made him one of its victims.

Voltaire's passionate dedication to the well-being of humanity and the essential rights of every individual to live freely according to his or her own beliefs was based upon unexplainable personal sentiment, and existed long before he worked out a philosophy to support it. This natural sentiment was the driving force of his life. He would not have lived long, however, had he not also had an innate talent for survival and a willingness to do whatever it took to stay alive.

He said he had no intention of being burned for his beliefs and no intention of not expressing them either. He was clever enough to live to the age of eighty-three and die peacefully in his own bed. How he managed this was by living in self-imposed exile a lot of the time, and beating his adversaries at their own game the rest of the time. His most dangerous and deadly attacks were published anonymously. Although everyone knew by their unique style and devastating wit that they could have come from no other hand but Voltaire's, no one could prove it. As his popularity grew and the establishment became shakier, his victims were content to let it go unproven.

Furthermore he was not above writing flattering, though totally false, things about rich and powerful people who were so relieved to escape his devastating ridicule that they gave him money and their protection. Voltaire did not see this as being at all in violation of his principles. He was never after individuals to start with. He was after the system. And he would use the creatures of the system any way he could to subvert the very foundations of their power. Only a fox, he realized, could survive in a forest full of foxes. Another thing that contributed to his continued well-being was his talent for making money, which made him rich and always able to pay his way out of situations he could not charm his way out of. His money came, to some extent, from plays, but even more so it was made by shrewd investments and through legacies left to him by people whose devotion he had cleverly cultivated in one way or another.

We have in Voltaire no saint, but a great hero nonetheless; not a holy man, but a man dedicated to wholeness, who in a very real way contributed to the healing of the consciousness of the whole world.

We will never really know what shaped his unique character and placed him in lonely and dangerous opposition to the world in which he lived. But his early life does provide us with some interesting material for speculation.

His father was a fearful man. He made an excellent living as a minor governmental functionary, an official notary. His job was to manage the financial business of the wealthy estate holders. He saw to it that his clients prospered, and in turn he lived well on their fortunes. So well, in fact, that he was a firm though timid supporter of the establishment, with unquestioning loyalty to the status quo in the affairs of both church and state. Like most of those who did well, he found it easy to turn his back on the plight of the many who did not do well and never could with things as they were.

Voltaire's mother died when he was six and seems to have had little influence on his development. However, a woman of a very different type did figure prominently in his young life. She was the celebrated Ninon de Lenclos, a client of the boy's father and a woman of great influence and decided opinions. She was, in fact, a rich— and therefore highly respected—courtesan, already seventy years old at the time of Voltaire's birth. Still beautiful, she may not have still been going strong, but she was still going, which is in itself a tribute to her singularity. She had come to be a woman of great kindness and generosity as a result, as one historian puts it, of having had "the felicity of being loved by three generations of Frenchmen." She took a proprietary interest in Voltaire when he was still an infant, because he was sickly. She saw to it that he received excellent medical care. When he proved that he was going to live to grow up, she counted him her creature and made it her business to see that plans were made and money set aside for him to get a good Christian education. It seems Ninon had developed a deeply religious turn of mind, possibly from having been loved by several priests in the course of her long career.

When the time came, the boy was given over to the Jesuits. His father's highest hope was to turn him into a priest. That hope was quickly dashed when the boy proved to be devoted neither to his religion nor to his studies. He was by no account stupid, but simply not interested in anything but making rhymes. The rhymes he made were beautifully done, but the sentiments they expressed were not at all well received. He used his seemingly natural talent to ridicule both the piety and the logic of the Jesuits, the government, and society at large. He was a serious problem at school, and all were relieved when he left at the age of seventeen. It was only after that that his real education began, along with his troubles.

Voltaire's life-long fight was against any form of intolerance and for all forms of ethical self-expression. The motto "I don't agree with a word you say, but I will defend to the death your right to say it" is attributed to him.

He saw all institutionalized religion as the great enemy of personal well-being, founded on fraud and superstition, kept alive by fear and moral cowardice, and spread by fanaticism. "Crush the Infamy" was a motto he used over and over again. He did not make the fine distinction between religion and its practice because he perceived its evil as being woven into its fabric. He set out to destroy the power of the church by breaking its hold over the human mind.

He wrote:

> To whom shall I submit my soul? Shall I be a Christian just because I come from London or Madrid? Shall I be a Muslim simply because I was born in Turkey? I ought to think only for myself. The choice of religion is my greatest interest. You adore God through Mohammed or through the Grand Lama, or through the Pope. How unfortunate! Adore God for your own reasons.

He urged people not to abandon God, but to base their belief and their religious practice entirely on reason and their own experience, independent of any priesthood, scripture, or revelation. While exiled in England, he developed a great admiration for the Quakers, whom he described as plain, honest people who lived without priesthood, sacraments, or creed, guided entirely by the Inner Light. These people, he felt, were the followers of the true spirit of Jesus Christ.

Institutionalized religion has always had an identity problem: it has always confused itself with God. To take exception to it is to question the existence of God. So people who do take such exception are readily labelled "atheist." Voltaire did not escape this label in his day, and even in modern times people who should know better still hang it on him.

He was by no means an atheist. He once remarked that if God did not exist we would have to invent Him, because we cannot live effectively without the sense of a higher authority. He did not question God. He was outraged by how poorly God was represented by institutionalized religions, of all kinds.

"We are intelligent beings," he wrote, "and intelligent beings cannot have been formed by a blind, brute, insensible being." So the failure of religion to see the goodness in people, to love them and respond positively to their needs, doubts and fears, as well as their weaknesses, indicates that religion is far from being God's creation.

Voltaire was too skeptical to adhere to any particular system of philosophy and too mercurial to set down one of his own. But there are certain important consistencies in his thinking that come together to give us a picture of the philosophical heart of the man.

First of all there is God, a Supreme Being, that is the source of all life and the governor of all the living. This he holds to be self-evident, observable in the natural order of things. This Supreme Being is not knowable by us because Its totality is beyond our imagination. However, we can know as much about God as we need to know to live an ever-improving life. We can grow in our understanding of God only if our mind is permitted to range free and is not rigidly committed to any theological system. Although all our power comes from God, God does not care how much of it or how little of it we help ourselves to. The Infinite is not diminished by our limitations, that is, does not suffer for our sins, and is not delighted by our achievements. All of our suffering comes from the way we use our minds, as does all of our glory.

Next, our happiness rests entirely on our ability to love ourselves and do justice to ourselves. Our sense of love and justice cannot be achieved at the expense of other people, but is realized through loving service and just regard for other people. We are enlarged and blessed and prospered by this more than by getting things from the world.

All earthly power, including government and religion, must be devoted to encouraging this kind of individual behavior, without which there can be nothing but human stagnation. People have within themselves the power to understand themselves correctly and the desire to direct their lives correctly. They must be left free to discover this for themselves. There is nothing to fear from allowing this, because bad ideas will never survive open and honest scrutiny, just as good ideas will always survive every kind of repression. When we try to control people, we never prevent progress, we simply delay it, and we do so at the terrible price of human misery and degradation with all the evil consequences that must naturally follow.

In 1792 when the forces of the French Revolution stormed the Bastille and turned loose its prisoners, Voltaire was resting in his grave. His work had come before and now was done. He had already ensured the success of a world-wide revolution of human thought by using his words to set us free from the Bastille of the fearful mind.

9

Transcendental Idealist

Immanuel Kant
(1724–1804)

SCHOPENHAUER wrote:

The chief jewel in the crown of Frederick the Great is Immanuel Kant. Such a man as Kant could not have held a salaried position under any other monarch on the globe at that time and have expressed the things that Kant did. A little earlier or a little later and there would have been no such person as Immanuel Kant. Rulers are seldom big men, but if they recognize and encourage big men they deserve the gratitude of mankind.

Frederick the Great was one of the last of the absolute monarchs in Europe. His power was in no way dependent upon the support of the church, so he was not obliged to promote any particular brand of theology. The Catholic church was nonexistent in his kingdom of Prussia, and the Lutheran state church was firmly under his thumb. Frederick's vast power at home rested entirely upon the wisdom of his rule. His people were secure and prosperous.

Frederick's protection from enemies abroad resided in his reputation for military genius and his highly visible and very powerful modern army, which he kept ever at the ready.

He was by no means a benign monarch. He demanded the total obedience of his subjects and complete personal loyalty from his friends. Fortunately, few found it difficult to conform to these standards, and most found it highly prosperous. Since his power did not rely on ignorance and superstition for its life, Frederick was able to dabble in new ideas. He delighted in this because he had a naturally curious turn of mind. New ideas, even those entirely inconsistent with the absolutism he practiced, always interested him. He not only permitted a wide range of opinion to be expressed at his court, but he patronized thinking men of every description. I say thinking *men* because Frederick's was a bachelor court. There were no women. He considered women to be distractions to serious thought. Aside from that, he personally preferred the company of men.

Voltaire found refuge at the Prussian court for several years. He freely aired his libertarian views and arguments against tyranny. Frederick admired the sharpness of his mind and the logic of his arguments. He loved to debate with him and was delighted by how thoroughly Voltaire's ideas frightened his rival, the King of France.

Immanuel Kant was born at Königsberg, the capital city of Prussia, and lived his entire eighty years without setting foot outside of the kingdom. For the first fifty-seven years of his life he was unknown outside Prussia. With the publication of *Critique of Pure Reason* in 1781, he became a world celebrity. This did not draw him away from home, but rather drew the attention of the world to Prussia, and Frederick was bursting with pride at his home-grown genius. The great king took the little philosopher to his heart, and for the remaining twenty years of Kant's life he was given every incentive to let his mind and pen flow freely.

Kant was an unlikely hero. Everything about him seemed to spell defeat. There is a popular belief that in order to excel one must have the right breaks. This keeps a lot of people very busy looking for the right opportunity or waiting for someone to give them a chance, instead of doing whatever can be done with whatever they already have. Had Immanuel Kant waited for the world to give him a break, he would have been broken by the world early on. Because from the beginning there was nothing about him that appeared very hopeful. On the face of it he was a prime candidate for either pity or ridicule depending on the temperament of the onlooker.

He was born into a poor working-class family. His father was a day laborer, a leather cutter, supporting seven children on his meager earnings. There was love in the home that always managed to override the family's financial difficulties. Both mother and father wanted the best for their children and demanded that the children prepare to go out and make something of themselves. The other six children were a normal and healthy lot: Immanuel was neither. He weighed five pounds at birth and grew into a weak, sickly, peculiar-looking child with a big bulging head, thin rickety legs, a concave chest, and one shoulder pitched significantly higher than the other. His physical growth stopped when he reached a bare five feet in height.

It became evident to his concerned parents that Immanuel would never be able to engage in honest work, so they decided he should become a preacher. Surely the good Lord would not deprive the child of both brawn *and* brains. If the size of his head was any measure he must certainly have more than enough brains to learn something.

At age sixteen he was packed off to the university where he was to remain for the rest of his life. He moved from student teacher up through the ranks to become its most distinguished professor. At first he was devoted to becoming a preacher and he learned his lessons well. He was soon sent out to preach in rural districts as a sort of student preacher. He took an immediate dislike to the practical application of his chosen profession, perhaps because he had to stand on a box to be seen above the pulpit.

He quickly arrived at this conclusion:

> *I stand on a box so as to impress the people by my height or to conceal my insignificant size. This is pretense, and a desire to carry out the idea that the preacher is bigger in every way than common people. I talk with God in intended prayer, but this looks as if I were on easy and familiar terms with the Deity. It is like those folk who claim to be on friendly terms with princes. If I do not know anything about God, why should I pretend to?*

We detect in his statement an honesty that is peculiar to youth and is too often left behind under the pressure of the adult world to grow up and be responsible. It was a trait that was to be fundamental to Kant's character all his life long. Perhaps it ran stronger in him to begin with, since neither his humble origins, his size, nor his appearance worked well to support any kind of pretentiousness.

At any rate, Kant soon abandoned his theological studies, telling his teacher he would be better off grooming young men who could impress people without standing on a box. His youthful turning away from the ministry set an entirely new direction to his life and liberated his mind from any kind of doctrinal limitation. He came to believe that the source of our power and the well of our goodness was not to be found in allegiance with any theological system or by any kind of formalized worship. For the last fifty years of his life he never entered a church. His record for nonattendance was threatened late in his career when he became chancellor of the university. On his installation he was required by tradition to lead a procession to the cathedral where formal religious services were to be held to mark the occasion. Everyone snickered, believing that at last he would be forced to enter. But he didn't. He led the procession to the door of the cathedral and then, pleading an urgent necessity, he left the others to enter and went around to the back of the cathedral where he relieved himself, and quietly went home.

Having ruled out his becoming the world's shortest preacher, he decided to prepare for a teaching career. He was a prize student and went on to become a professor of logic and metaphysics, highly respected by his colleagues and much loved by his students. The world has come to know Immanuel Kant only through the writings of his later years, which though brilliant, are heavy, formal, and complex. But those who knew him as students leave the impression that in the classroom he was both an inspiration and a delight. His wit was keen, but rising from true humor, not bitterness. It was often directed towards himself, though he also used it quite effectively against all sorts of human pretension. His students always expected him to poke holes in high-flown pieties. And he always obliged them with remarks like this: "The statement that man is the noblest work of God was never made by anyone but man, and must therefore be taken with a grain of salt."

As a teacher, Kant persistently directed his students to look to themselves for their authority and not to the experts around them, who made a living from getting people to believe that they knew what was best for them, and could tell them how to think and what to do. He made a particular point of unmasking what he considered the fraudulent authority of clergymen, lawyers, and physicians, whose reach, he believed, had always exceeded their grasp.

He believed that a Supreme Power was evident, and our belief in it a necessity if we are to live sanely. He did not believe that the Supreme Power picked out some individuals to function as Its authority. Most people, he thought, turn to religion not to learn the truth but to escape from it, as truth is generally unpopular. Preachers, he said, are the wage earners of our religions. They will not get paid if they do not tell people what they want to hear. So preaching quite naturally turns to sophistication and hypocrisy in its efforts to manipulate the people into supporting the preachers.

He viewed physicians in much the same way: they cared more about pleasing their patients than telling them the truth. Their objective was not to teach the patient what he must do to maintain health, but to help him avoid the natural consequences of the sickness that the patient himself had invited.

"No doctor with a family to support" he said, "can afford to tell his patient that his symptoms are no token of disease, but proof of health, for dead men don't have them.'' Our symptoms, painful as they may be, are nature's way of warning us and showing her efforts to restore our natural health. Kant insisted that physicians treat symptoms, not diseases, and that the treatment quite often causes disease. So, although some disease is caused by ignorance and careless living, some is also caused by medical treatment.

The lawyer's business, he said, is not to protect the client's interest, but to advance his own, not to solve simple problems, but to complicate them so that his legal services and fees will be ongoing. Their objective is not to see that justice is done, but to figure out how to evade justice. People support this effort lavishly, because in truth when people say they want justice, they really mean revenge.

Kant was not trying to turn his public against clergymen, physicians, or lawyers. He was never out to get anyone. He made it clear that these professions functioned as they did in response to what people wanted and were willing to support. They were evidence of people's refusal to recognize their own authority and face up to the responsibility for the character of their consciousness and the conduct of their lives.

His own experiences with doctors certainly fed the flames of his conviction. From the beginning, medical opinion offered him little hope of a long or productive life. His puny, misshapen body was medically alarming. The doctors advised him to be as physically inactive as possible, even to abandon all study and all hope of ever being anything but an invalid. There was no one in his life who encouraged him otherwise. So as a very young man he had to choose to accept the seemingly overwhelming weight of medical opinion and lie down and die, or reject it, stand up, and live. He chose the latter.

He got the idea that air was the essence of life and strength. If he would breathe more deeply, drawing in the enlivening air of life, he would be relieved of the pains of his malformed body and the headaches that assaulted his oversized skull. He would then think clearly as well as draw strength into his muscles and joints. He developed a daily routine of going outdoors, in every kind of weather, and walking rapidly while breathing deeply and rhythmically through his nose. He built these walks up to a distance of four miles a day, up and down the street on which he lived. His neighbors scoffed at first but in time came to view the habit with gentle amusement, which in time turned to admiration. He did this daily, from youth until a year before his death at age eighty, long after some of the original scoffers had been laid to rest. He thus created for himself a long and able existence using a healing technique that was supported by nothing but his own belief.

This firmness in following his own ideas when there were no more promising ones available saved his life. His tendency to do this in all things developed the character and the mind that were to bring him to lasting greatness. He knew where the power of life came from and how to receive it. From his own experience he gives us the dictum, ''Mind is supreme, and the Universe is but the reflected thought of God.''

After the publication of *Critique of Pure Reason,* he was famous and received invitations to go to all the cultural centers of Europe so that his great mind could be further probed. But Kant went nowhere. He had not the least interest in exploring new places. It was not that he lacked a universal view or a sense of adventure, but he regarded the exploration of his mind as the only real adventure, and that he could pursue endlessly while staying comfortably at home. "The imagination hath a stage upon which all scenes are played," he wrote. He went further:

> *Time and Space have no existence apart from the Mind. There is no such thing as sound unless there is an ear to receive the vibration. Things and places, matter and substance, come under the same law, and exist only as mind creates them.*

Kant's body of philosophy is described by scholars as "transcendental idealism." He wanted to translate intellectual ideas into practical action. Only this way, he believed, were ideals useful to the individual and of proven value.

We have two lives, he theorized: the life of the body in the world and the life of the mind that is beyond the world and out of the confines of human experience. If we live only in the world, we live a limited and constantly diminishing life. But the world of mind is a realm of new ideas, and our mind is free to bring them into the world of form and so improve its possibilities. We lift ourselves up out of ordinary experience by raising our minds to extraordinary ideas and learning how to put them into practice.

His writings along this line are voluminous and complex. But they can be represented by this simplified explanation. According to Kant, the four great questions in life are:

"Who am I?"
"What am I?"
"What can I do?"
"What can I know?"

The answer to number four is, "I cannot know anything." We become wise, as Socrates suggested, only when we know that we know nothing for sure. The answer to number four, then, answers number one and number two, leaving only number three for us to consider: "What can I do?"

"What can I do?" then resolves into "What must I do?" because, unless we are ready to commit ourselves to what we can, in order to improve the quality of our existence, there is no point in asking the question to begin with. This is, I think, a point that cannot be too frequently or too strongly made, particularly to those professional searchers for truth that fly from book to book, class to class, and guru to guru to find answers that they wouldn't put into action even if they were not too caught up in ego to hear them. Everybody, no matter how dark or limited their present circumstances appear to be, has something that can be done. Usually it is something as dreary and painful as the present circumstances. But nevertheless, if it can be done it must be done before a level of higher experience can be achieved, because even the highest and most beautiful thought is only a thought, and is only of transient value unless we can apply it to our present condition. As a thought it may be enticing or challenging but in any case only a distraction, never a solution.

Kant proposed four things that we must do: We must eat, work, associate with our kind, and rest. It is not the mere doing of these things that raises us up above ordinary experience, it is *how* we do them.

What is the quality of thought, the idea, that we bring to these functions?

Do we eat wisely or stupidly? Joyfully or compulsively? The consciousness that directs us in our eating determines the quality of life that is produced by this essential human function. It brings health or happiness, energy or stupor, right weight or corpulence to our bodies. This applies not only to what we eat, but how much, how often, and with what attitude. Each person knows within himself how to fulfill the eating function in exactly the right way for himself. There is no mystery to it, only a lot of confusion around it. One of the greatest confusions is the belief—very popular these days—that a person can't help himself when it comes to food, unless it's to help himself to more chocolate cake.

But the truth is, if you can't help yourself, certainly no one else can, although there will always be plenty of people who tell you they can, and merely help themselves to your money in the process. There are many other people these days who respond to the demands of their appetites by going to the other extreme with something that approaches religious fervor. They deny themselves, starve themselves, and comfort themselves with the notion that they are not only physically healthier, but spiritually more advanced than their fellow beings. Some of the more extreme cases have talked themselves into such a limited acceptable menu that they cannot dine out in society. They think they are rising above unwholesome appetites when they are only alienating themselves from their natural environment.

Do we work happily? Is our object of work to produce value, to tender a good service, and to constantly improve in our chosen field? Is it our chosen field or merely some job we have fallen into or grappled to get for purposes of prestige or for fear of starvation? Healthful work follows personal ideal, not dire necessity or the need for respectability.

Do we associate with our kind? Or do we associate with whoever is passing through or making camp in front of our face at the present time? Do we seek out or hang on to people for reasons other than those of natural affinity? If our lives are filled with people for artificial reasons, then our relationships are merely little dramas that always end up the same way, and are always repeated on another stage. Some of them are life-long dramas. None of them let us rise above the artificiality of their scripts.

What about rest? Many people don't even know how. Rest means more than falling into bed at a certain hour or taking a hectic two-week vacation every year. Rest is not simply a matter of sleeping. That's why so many people wake up exhausted. Nor is it a matter of getting away from it all. It has to do with having the good sense, and the courage, to put things aside, to know when to do this, and to know you can do this without having the world cave in on you.

So many of us live in reaction to ideas that make no sense but are well-supported by society, industry, religion, and our own own unexplored attitudes. We take our authority from beyond our inner knowing. In return we do get what the world has to offer, but we don't get what life has to offer, and they are not the same. The world is old and finished, but life is eternally new, and new life presents itself only within the consciousness of the individual.

If we are to find the path to new life, we must make ourselves free to pursue our individuality. If we are to live in a better world, we must let other people be free to do the same.

Somehow Immanuel Kant worked this out for himself, maybe because he had to in order to survive at all. It may or may not be necessary to your survival or mine, but it is certainly necessary to making our survival worth the effort.

10

The Prophet
of Greater Possibility

Ralph Waldo Emerson
(1803–1882)

B Y THE TIME of Emerson, the natural liberty of the
individual and the right to form and follow personal
beliefs was fundamental to modern philosophy and was
gaining popularity throughout the western world. It had
given birth to the democratic ideal in politics. The absolute power of monarchs and the exclusive privilege of the
aristocracy was rapidly becoming a thing of the past in
Europe. A new era of constitutional government, with
power passing into the hands of elected officials, was
emerging even where kings were still tolerated. Some
European countries were on their way to out-and-out
Republicanism. This form of government had already
been established in the new United States of America,
where it was working with increasing effectiveness. In
Europe state religions were still the order of the day.

Although these churches certainly maintained a privileged position with the government and were accepted by most of the population, their political and economic power was on the decline. Their direct power over government was being systematically reduced. Their legal right to abuse people for theological reasons was disappearing.

In the United States the Constitution provided for no state religion and no legal recourse against the practice of any religion. So, in effect, it granted freedom of worship as it granted political freedom.

This was a great step forward. But it did not mean that personal freedom of conscience was easy to practice or that people had suddenly become highly tolerant of others different from themselves. It only meant that people could no longer legally persecute or be persecuted by other people on the basis of a difference of belief.

The vast majority of people in the new United States were Anglo-Saxon in origin and some brand of Protestant in religion. This was the respected pedigree. People of other nationalities, races, and religions could not legally be abused, but they were not socially accepted and so had little popular support in the exercise of their rights and in their reach for excellence.

Of course, the black slaves brought in from Africa had no rights at all. In failing to rule out the institution of slavery, the Constitution had legalized this inhuman practice, which was totally inconsistent with the constitutional ideal. It was a barbarism that even the most autocratic regimes of Europe had stopped practicing ages before.

Ralph Waldo Emerson lived in this age, and his life was devoted to further advancing the expression of individual freedom. However, his writings and lectures were not so much directed at convincing people that they had a right to their individuality as at convincing people that they had a moral obligation to boldly express it without fear of failure or retribution. He didn't want to teach us religion. We already had more than enough of that. He wanted to make each one of us aware that God was on our side, and that all the power of the universe would support our honest and loving self-expression and absolutely compensate us for any loss or injury incurred in the process. Our problems, he believed, do not come from what other people do to us or fail to do for us, but from our own failure to follow our own conscience. He wrote, "The difficulty is that we do not make a world of our own, but fall into institutions already made." Obedience to others, conformity to established ideas, had never yet brought humankind to its highest good. The time had come for the individual to be an individual if he or she was to experience a personally satisfying life. He believed every person was created for such a life, and that we honored God, ourselves, and our fellow human beings only to the extent that we created such a life for ourselves. Human institutions may seem to oppose individual expression, but God supports it, and Divine Power will always obliterate all human opposition to it. He tells us, "That is always best that gives me to myself. The sublime is excited in me by the great Stoical doctrine, 'Obey Thyself.' That which shows God in me, fortifies me."

"What he taught others to be he was himself." This high praise comes from the great Oliver Wendell Holmes. It explains why Emerson, in both his essays and his public lectures, compelled serious attention and affection from the general public. Here was a man talking from experience, not from mere theory, and recognizing in his audience the intelligence and courage to rise up to this challenge. He made his case clearly and powerfully without abusing his audience. His challenge was never accusative, but always inviting. He could express absolute conviction without contempt, because his conviction came from unimpeachable personal experience. What he urged others to overcome, he had overcome in himself. What he urged them to accomplish, he had accomplished for himself. He was obviously not trying to win his audience over to a cause, but urging them to be their own cause.

Emerson's father had not been a successful man. He died when Emerson was still a child, and the family was left without resources. His mother was faced with the task of raising a bunch of young children with no wage earner in the house and no wealthy family member to rely on. In those days most women were not equipped to be wage earners, and besides there was no place for them in industry or business. A decent woman in Mrs. Emerson's position was expected to carry on nevertheless and do a respectable job of raising her family. She devoted herself to this objective, and for all the years ahead she and her children survived on the odds and ends of charity and friends.

In addition to poverty, Waldo was confronted with a weak constitution. He had lung problems that stayed with him all of his long life. His vision was poor, and he developed an embarrassing facial tic.

Along with his brothers, the boy worked for his education, applied himself diligently to his studies and at last qualified to be a teacher.

He fell deeply in love with a young woman. After a patient and passionate courtship, they married, and it seemed that he had found his perfect mate. She died six months later, leaving him devastated.

Several years later he married again, forming a thoroughly good and stable relationship with a woman who knew how to care for him, and he cared for her greatly. But the passion of romance and young love was never to come to him again. His firstborn son became his real delight, seeming to somehow fill the terribly lonely void left in him by the death of his first love. At the age of six, the boy died. Once again, Emerson was devastated.

"I am defeated all the time, yet to victory am I born," he wrote. And so he was. And so, he knew, we all are. He had his victorious life, though it was never without its great disappointments, its challenges, and its sacrifices. Unlike so many people, he realized that our misfortunes do not separate us from life's power and are never legitimate excuses for not living fully, sanely, and productively. This realization lies at the heart of all Emerson's teaching.

As a school teacher he could not find the fulfillment that he sought, though he was greatly respected by his superiors and well loved by his students. He regarded the educational system of the day as inhibiting true education. Its intent was to program old ideas, not to draw forth new ones, and this he viewed not as true education at all. It was not geared to the development of the mind but devoted to making the student a repository of past ideas and stock attitudes. It discouraged genuine curiosity and gave rewards for being able to recite material that the student had no real interest in. He held that students learned more from the books that were excluded from the curricula— books that excited their real interest—than from books included that inspired resistance. He thought student tests had no educational value and were really only tools to compel surface learning. They created no scholarship, only a spirit of unhealthy competition.

He could not change the system, so he had to find the courage to leave it. To stay on would lead to nothing but ongoing strife, as he could not abandon his ideals. He had the integrity not to continue taking money from a system that he did not respect and could not resist subverting.

His next career was the ministry. It was a likely choice. His family on both sides had produced distinguished New England clergymen for several generations. Besides, he had a true interest in religion. Even when he was a child, people observed in him what they called "a spiritual turn of mind."

After attending Harvard Divinity School, he became pastor of a prestigious Unitarian church in Boston. His congregation loved him, his gentleness, his wit. It seemed that he was comfortably set for life.

But he was not comfortable. For one thing, he found that he disliked formalized public prayer. He considered it not at all genuine communion with the Infinite, but rather an attempt to make a pious impression on one's neighbors. He also detested the obligation of paying formal calls on members of his congregation, listening to small-talk, gossip, and uninformed critiques of last Sunday's service that reflected more personal ignorance than spiritual insight. Although he loved people in principle, he disliked the company of most people as individuals, because their conversation showed their pettiness. He was bored by them and embarrassed for them.

But more than all of that, he found it more and more difficult to preach what his congregation was paying to hear, since much of it was not what he himself believed. He could not be happy as the servant of any creed. Unitarianism was, to be sure, free of much of the cruel nonsense of older theologies but, in his opinion, still subject to more nonsense than he cared to defend or promote. He longed to speak only the truth as he perceived it, and to be free to alter his views on anything when his unfolding understanding led him to new conclusions.

So in time he left the ministry and devoted himself to writing his essays and giving public lectures as an independent thinker. In other words, since he could not work happily for others, he had the courage to go into business by himself. He gave himself freedom, and in his freedom he found his place—and fame and fortune as well.

Emerson's central concern was the individual's relationship to the Universe. He viewed God as Universal Intelligence intent on creating through each individual the best that the individual could conceive for himself or herself. He viewed every person as connected to God's flow of creative ideas at soul level. All people are thus established in essential wisdom, and all are capable of personalizing that wisdom through a process of creative thinking.

He tells us this:

> *A little consideration of what takes place around us every day would show us that a higher law than that of our will regulates events; that our painful labors are unnecessary and futile; that only in easy, simple spontaneous action are we strong. . . . Place yourself in the middle of the stream of power and wisdom which animates all whom it floats, and you are without effort impelled to truth, to right, and a perfect contentment.*

Creative thinking, then, is not a matter of hanging on to old ideas. Nor is it a matter of following other people's directions. It is a matter of, first, realizing there is within yourself something that knows, and then letting your mind be receptive to its inner knowing. "All progress," he said, "is an unfolding, like the vegetable bud. You have first an instinct, then an opinion, then a knowledge, as a plant had root, bud, and fruit. Trust the instinct to the end, though you can render no reason."

"We are never without a pilot," he tells us. "When we know not how to steer, and dare not hoist a sail, we can drift. The current knows the way though we do not. The ship of heaven knows the way and will not accept a wooden rudder."

So when we seem not to know, something inside us does know. It is our instinct or intuition. We need not force a conclusion and cannot will ourselves into productive action. The thing to do is be still and let our inner knowing guide us until we can once again confidently take control.

> *What your heart thinks is great, is great. The soul's emphasis is always right. . . . A man should learn to detect and watch that gleam of light which flashes across his mind from within.*

So in Emerson's view our power is truly within ourselves, along with the authority to draw upon it. Not only do we have a God-given right to independent thought and action, we have a God-given obligation to exercise it. We suffer when we fail to do this and flourish as we learn to do it. Our suffering is not afflicted upon us from on high, but created by our own failure to use what God has given us. Our success does not depend upon the protection, regard, or encouragement of other people, but on our commitment to use the power that only we possess.

The great obstacle to our right action is fear based on

ignorance. We think we must conform to the world in order to get along in the world. But the world offers us nothing for our conformity but its approval, and the place and power we seek can come only from our own self-approval, from the satisfaction of knowing that we are being true to ourselves. The power within us that urges individuality will also find a way to reward it, though all the world seems to oppose us, because it is the unopposable power of God.

Emerson recognized that all persons do not appear to be equally equipped for life. But he wrote of a Law of Compensation that worked within us all to provide strength to offset every weakness: that what is lacking one place will be made up for in another. It is a balancing power that works to bring every person in line for the pursuit of his or her own success. So that if the individual will work to get clear on his or her objective, the Law will find a way to fulfill it, no matter how limited he or she appears to be.

Thinking America responded to Emerson. The character of his life and the power and clarity of his spoken and written word gave wide public appeal to his message of achievement through the power of personal sanity. People began to understand that the great American Revolution had not ended with the achievement of free institutions. The next and logical step was to create a nation populated by free minds who would break through the barriers of social and economic injustice so that no person would be defined or limited by origin, or class, or religious affiliation. In time, people would further realize that no person should be defined or limited by gender or race or any other circumstances they did not for themselves create.

A century later, Martin Luther King, Jr. called upon

us to measure people only by the content of their character. Emerson might well have expressed this same sentiment, as the freedom to achieve depended entirely upon the quality of our own consciousness.

Emerson did not go unmaligned during his lifetime. He was regularly attacked by many great theologians of the day—whose names are now forgotten—as a fool, an infidel, even an atheist. The pro-slavery people hated him because he detested their "filthy institution." The abolitionists hated him because he detested their mindless clamoring for war, which he regarded as mankind's greatest infamy; it was the answer to no problem and the cause of endless misery.

> *All violence, all that is dreary and repels, is not power, but the absence of power. . . . The key to every man is his thought. Sturdy and defiant though he look, he has a helm which he obeys. . . . He can only be reformed by showing him a new idea which commands his own.*

He could not be moved by those who sought to coerce him into a show of respect for that which he could not respect, including "the dear old doctrines of the church." Nor could he be bullied into giving his endorsement to those who would make war against anyone—even for the most just cause. He taught, "There is a remedy for every wrong and a satisfaction for every soul," but these things were to be found only in peace and mutual respect.

His challenge to us was to find them under these conditions and to be undeterred, as he was, by the clamor and demands of the world around us. The world has never had the right solutions. That's why it keeps making the same mistakes over and over again.

Emerson never responded in kind to his critics. He saw no point in fanning the flames that reached out to consume him. He granted them their point of view and stuck to his own, putting his full energy into what he believed. It was not the easy way, but it was in his view the only way to remain credible. He tells us, "It is easy in the world to live after the world's opinion; it is easy in solitude to live after your own; but the great man is he who, in the midst of the crowd, keeps with perfect sweetness the independence of his solitude."

He lived a long life that, year after year, brought him more and more love and prosperity of every kind. He made the life he wanted, paid for it, enjoyed it, and left us more than a body of great literature. He left us a powerful example of a life well lived.

11

Mental Evolutionist

Herbert Spencer
(1820–1903)

HERBERT SPENCER was an only child. His mother died when he was quite young, so his memory of her was largely imaginative and highly idealistic. It was based upon information about the good woman from the lips of those who loved her dearly and, therefore, grossly exaggerated her virtues and totally ignored any possible inadequacies. The boy came to regard his mother as a saint and to equate womanly virtue with saintliness, which was properly worshipped only from afar. Not surprisingly, Herbert Spencer never married. He was thus able to hold onto his illusion all his life. It was the only area of his life in which he lacked objectivity. In all other things he was a keen observer of facts and a remoreseless critic.

Spencer's father was schoolmaster in the then-small town of Derby, England. Father and son lived above the schoolhouse. Spencer remarked in later life that he was unable to remember a time when he was not in school. The widowed schoolmaster carried his infant son in his arms as he taught his daily classes. As soon as the child could understand, the father began teaching him both upstairs and downstairs.

Fortunately, the schoolmaster approached learning as a joyful experience and was inclined to present all subjects as games rather than chores. He himself never tired of learning and so did not infect his students with the idea that education was either boring or difficult. His only close adult association following the death of his wife was with his brother, a scholarly clergyman who visited weekly. The two men spent their time together advancing their own education. They were interested in absolutely everything—mathematics, literature, nature, politics—and explored these things together in hours of conversation, reading, and wondering. Young Herbert was included from the beginning. As he grew, he became an active third party in all these deliberations. The men had no idea that they were grooming one of the greatest thinkers of the century. They were merely sharing the best of themselves with the one they loved best. Neither of them lived long enough to see Herbert Spencer rise to greatness.

In later years, Spencer became appalled at the limited knowledge of even those who had been sent to the "best schools" of the day and at the general apathy toward continued education that afflicted the majority of Englishmen at all levels of society. He felt it was responsible for all the political stupidity and social injustice of his day, and believed it was correctable only by reforming the educational system from top to bottom, to make learning a joy rather than a chore and a bore.

He wrote:

The man to whom in boyhood information came in dreary tasks, along with threats of punishment, is unlikely to be a student in after years; while those to whom it came in natural forms, at the proper times, and who remember its facts as not only interesting in themselves, but as a long series of gratifying successes, are likely to continue through life that self-instruction begun in youth.

True learning, he felt, centered on the developed capacity for objective observation and persistent questioning. The object of the questioning was not to get a final answer, but to secure enough information to lead one on to more intelligent questioning. The ability to pose the right questions was the key to learning, because the right answers naturally flowed when the right questions were posed.

Though the elder Spencer was able to lavish much love and wisdom on his son, he was unable to do much for him financially. An excellent schoolmaster was paid no more than a poor one even in those days. So young Herbert Spencer was not to be sent on for university education. At seventeen he was looking for a job and promptly found a position as an apprentice to the surveyor on the London-Birmingham Railway. His department had to do with railway construction and the young man's inventive mind and talent for mathematics soon came to the attention of his superiors. At their urging, Herbert conceived of shorter and more efficient methods for constructing bridges and culverts. He was duly promoted and urged to write articles for trade journals explaining these methods and other new concepts in civil engineering. These articles were respectfully received, but he was not paid for them. They were intended to bring prestige, not cash. But Herbert needed cash and had little interest in gaining prestige in a field of work that already bored him. But now he knew he could make himself understood in writing. So he decided to put his hand to writing about what truly interested him and to see if he couldn't get paid for it as well.

At age twenty-one he began submitting articles of a political nature to *The Non-Conformist,* a publication that was everything its name suggests. Every issue was filled with articles taking exception to just about everything that the British establishment of the day held dear—except, of course, Queen and Crown, which was off-limits to public criticism.

In one of these articles Spencer put forth a daring hypothesis concerning the evolution of the soldier. It went something like this: When primitive man evolved out of the Stone Age and began to live in villages, the oldest and wisest man of the village became chief. The chief's function was to settle disputes, see to the welfare of the villagers, and protect them from wrongdoers. There were always a few characters who could not operate within the parameters of this primitive civilization—being inclined to abuse others and steal from them, and disinclined to honest work. They were either run out of the village or they fled to escape punishment. They found refuge in the wilderness, banding together to escape capture and to conduct organized raids on the village to secure their living. Robbery was their commerce and they became very proficient at it. Finally they became such a problem that the village came to terms with them. The village would pay them tribute in exchange for their protection against other robber brigades. The tribute would be collected as a tax on the industry of the honest folk of the village. In this manner the idea of a standing army became part of civilized life. Its function was to protect the community from outside attacks and to enforce the government's taxation of the people for the support of the army. In time the army was used to support all the government's policies, domestic and foreign, and to maintain the power of the government whether people like it or not.

Spencer's hypothesis came very close to treason in a day when Great Britain was awash with adoration of its army and navy and relying on the might of both to extend its influence to all parts of the world. His additional hypothesis about the evolution of the priest put him in further danger of being considered an enemy of the realm.

According to Spencer, the priest had originated as a "holy man" who was given to the pursuit of religious ecstasy and took himself away from the mundane life and work of the village to live in the wilderness. These individuals discovered that, despite the exalted status they had assumed for themselves, they grew hungry. So they periodically returned to civilization to preach, to do good, and to beg. They claimed to have a special relationship with whatever deity was believed in at the time and to be able to influence that deity on behalf of people who would feed, clothe, and shelter them. They found special favor with the soldier, who tended to be more ignorant and consequently given more to superstition than most. And, of course, the soldier was able to enforce the support of the priest at no extra cost to himself, since it was not by his labors that food, clothing, shelter, and other necessities of life were produced. So the soldier protected the priest and the priest absolved the soldier and guaranteed him success and safety in battle. In time, priest and soldier came into shared domination of the lives of the people, one dictating man's place in this world, one dictating man's place in the next.

These articles, and others which followed concerning society and government, were later expanded into lengthy essays and published as a book, *Social Statics, or the Conditions Essential to Human Happiness.* It was Spencer's first great work. It was published at his own expense, probably because no publisher would put money behind anything so bold and so radical. It suggested revolution at a time when revolution was far from the minds of most Englishmen, then basking in the prosperity of Great Britain's colonial power and glory.

At the heart of *Social Statics* was a plea for the liberty of the individual. The British monarch no longer reigned supreme, but the British class system did, and the government was dedicated to keeping it so. The individual was born to his lot, be it abundant or meager. No person could rise higher, no matter how great his talents nor how hard he worked. In the case of the upper classes, no person could drop lower, regardless of how stupid or indolent he was. The term "upstart" was in popular usage, being applied to anyone who displayed talent or industry that might let him rise above his "station" in life.

Spencer proposed that this system was essentially corrupt. It was not merely unfair to individuals, but would in time weaken the entire nation by depriving it of the talent and industry necessary to its growth. Government should be looking beyond social limitations and lending its support to all people who truly have something to offer, seeing that they are brought forward and justly rewarded. Instead, government was using its power to judge people by the circumstances of their birth and persecuting them for their individuality if the way they chose to express life was seen as a threat to established attitudes.

He said that the government had no business scrutinizing the life or the beliefs of the individual. Government is for people, not people for government. All opinion should be respected, because civilization evolves only by the expression of opinion. To have a wrong opinion is better than having no opinion at all. All people, he said, wish to do what is best and eventually will, if left alone to work things out for themselves. All human growth occurs through constant practice and frequent mistakes. Therefore, people must be allowed the privilege of living from their own ideas and given the right to be wrong. He saw nothing to fear from this. In his mind, the limit of individual liberty was clear: it came only at the point where one person's rights actually interfered with another's.

By Spencer's reckoning, the government is not to think for the people. The age-old argument that the few know better than the many is spurious. It is the same as the slaveholder's argument that he can take better care of people than people can take care of themselves. Such a person's rightful obligation is to teach people how to take care of themselves and leave them free to do it, not to make his living off of their present inadequacy. To thrive by holding others in bondage is to make a slave of all. Both slaveholder and slave cease to be free people, because a person has only as much freedom as his own talents will bring him.

There was little difference to Spencer between enslavement of the body and enslavement of the mind. Both interfered with nature's law of evolution, and everything contrary to nature could only bring pain, disease, and ultimate destruction.

The first printing of *Social Statics* was limited by the size of Spencer's purse to 750 copies. It was by no means a bestseller. People were not at all ready for this kind of thinking. Perhaps it's just as well. If it had been widely read, who knows what misery it might have brought down on the author? It could well have been the end of him; and that would have been a great loss, for he was only thirty-one and had another fifty years or so to give us.

Six years after the publication there were 500 copies still unsold. If the author was disappointed, he didn't show it, and he certainly wasn't deterred by it. He did not need popular acclaim to support his opinion. He remarked, "I am glad the public is taking plenty of time to fully digest my work before passing judgment on it. Of all things, hasty criticisms are to be avoided."

The book was, however, read by one person who was consequently drawn into Spencer's life in a very special way. Her name was Mary Ann Evans. She had come to London from the country, determined to make a career as a writer. She sought out Spencer and, to their mutual delight, they discovered they had everything in common including a love of literature, a commitment to radical political ideas, and a passion for personal independence at all costs. A strong relationship developed between them. They delighted in each other and were together daily— though apparently not nightly, for physical love did not seem to come about between them.

Herbert's passion may not have extended to the boudoir, but Mary Ann's did. So in time she ran off to the continent with another man. He was not the mental equal of Spencer, but Mary Ann realized she was that herself. What she needed was something she didn't have, and which her friend Herbert did not seem likely to give. She lived with the man for the rest of her life, and with his love and support became the great writer that she aspired to be— known to the world as George Eliot.

Spencer was for a while devastated by her departure, but in time resumed his career, becoming more brilliant and more productive than ever. It seems that George Eliot's career took off when she round romance, and Herbert Spencer's did the same when he was relieved of the challenge of providing it. Spencer lived alone in second-class boarding houses to the end of his days. He had many admirers, but no intimate friends. His great passion was poured entirely into his work.

Spencer's speculations concerning human development through a process of evolution predated Darwin's theories by several years. He presented the idea of evolution as being superior to the belief that we came into being by a single act of God and always had been as we now appeared to be. He pointed out that there was absolutely no scientific evidence supporting the creationist point of view but a great deal of scientific evidence supporting evolutionism. The church, of course, subscribed to creationism as the only explanation for the origin of human life and indeed all life on the planet. Everything was created as it now appeared to be, and consequently everything would always be as it now appeared to be. Not a very hopeful view of our prospects to be sure, but this is what the Bible said. At least, it is what the church had always understood the Bible to say. And since nobody but the church could interpret the Bible correctly, this must be the unquestionable truth.

The accounts of creation in the early book of Genesis clearly describe exactly how it all came about. At the time, the book of Genesis was believed to have been written by Moses himself. Since then, biblical scholars of all persuasions have come to realize this is an impossibility. However, most Bible-based religions still teach it as fact, as they have never allowed scientific evidence to alter their established ideas.

If the Bible described creation that way, they argued, then that's the way it had to be. If this Mosaic account were not true, then the Bible itself would be untrue. And, of course, since the church assumed that its authority was based on the Bible, the church would no longer be a credible source of spiritual truth and have any legitimate authority over human existence.

The point they missed was that the church had lost its credibility centuries earlier, and its authority had not been legitimate since that time. Its status in the world had been largely secured by fear and superstition, which it had so skillfully implanted in the human mind, often using physical force.

In Spencer's view, we could not follow our natural process of evolution by clinging to ideas of ourselves that were false to begin with and served now only to justify the existence of a pernicious, self-serving church institution.

In his essay on *Manners and Fashions* he put it this way:

> *Forms, ceremonies, and even beliefs are cast aside only when they become hindrances—only when some finer and better plan has been formed; and they bequeath to us all the good that was in them. The abolition of tyrannical laws has left the administration of justice not only unimpaired, but purified. Dead and buried creeds have not carried down with them the essential morality they proclaimed, which still exists, uncontaminated by the sloughs of superstition. And all that there is of justice, kindness, beauty . . . will live perennially when the forms themselves have been repudiated and forgotten.*

So Spencer saw nothing to fear in repudiating the ancient and primitive explanation in Genesis as to how life came to be. Life would still be life. Man would still be man, and all that is good and true would remain good and true. Not coming from the authority of the church or the Bible to begin with, it could not suffer or be lost with the passing of the church or the Bible. All right answers existed before Bible or church, and the whole truth did not reside in either or depend upon either for its existence.

One of Spencer's most valuable concepts he expressed as the "Art of Mutation or Brain Building." All thoughts, he said, were registered in the brain where they created brain cells, which were structured to reflect the nature of the thought that created them. These brain cells functioned by sending out vibrations to all organs of the body, causing these organs to produce substances that were either toxic or energizing, with either disease or health as the result.

One could ensure continued health of the body, he speculated, by seeing that one's mind dealt only in health, and in loving, generous ideas. The mind that was fixed on ideas of hate, fear, and revenge was a diseased mind that in time would produce a diseased body. All thoughts, he argued, affect primarily the one thinking them, and no person can escape the inevitable consequences of the content of his or her mind.

To live healthfully, then, the individual must be committed to the mangagement of his or her own thought, developing the habit of not dealing with any kind of injurious ideas for any reason whatsoever.

He once again found an opportunity to take the church to task, saying that it should stop preaching to people in terms of the devil, hell, and damnation. Such ideas produced only fear, and resulted only in disease, never in the uplifting of the mind or the body.

As Spencer grew older, he became quite eccentric. One of his most amusing and outrageous eccentricities reflected his absolute belief in the destructive power of negative ideas: he began carrying a set of earmuffs on his person. When the conversation around him took what he considered to be a negative turn, he would unceremoniously put the earmuffs on, thus showing his disapproval of the negativity and sparing himself any effort to refute it. Because, after all, refutation is a form of participation.

At the time of his death at age eighty-three, Herbert Spencer had survived all of the fury that his ideas had set swirling around him and had come to be widely regarded as one of England's greatest philosophers. In a less civilized time or in a less civilized place his life would surely have been much shorter, nor would he have died in peace. But the mind of the race, though still barely able to see his great light without squinting, was by this time enlightened enough to keep him out of the clutches of those who would destroy him.

The Church of England, one of his great natural enemies, unable to deprive him of his rights while he lived, at last managed to do so after his death. He was not only denied burial in Westminster Abbey, along with England's other greats, but his body was assigned burial in unconsecrated ground.

And there Herbert Spencer rests, in peace and dignity.

12

Renaissance Man
Albert Schweitzer
(1875–1965)

THE NAME Albert Schweitzer is a household word. It stands for a selfless love that surpasses all understanding. We all know that this man devoted his life to the healing of natives in the remote jungles of Africa. We admire him greatly for it, but don't usually understand why he did it or how. The answer to that question is to be found in understanding the consciousness of the man. And that is well worth understanding, because it will bring to us a great gift of freedom. It is the freedom to fearlessly pursue our own noble instincts and so raise ourselves up from a life of struggling to do what is necessary for survival, to a life of doing what really pleases the soul. All of us want to live and to give more greatly than most of us will ever be able to do. But it is not the problems of the world or the circumstances in our environment that bar us from this greater experience. It is the ignorance that leads us to believe that the ideal life is a life of recreation rather than creative action, and the timidity that makes us reject our greater ideas before they have a chance to explain themselves to us.

We will never know for sure what took place in Schweitzer's life that enabled him to develop the most treasured commodities that life can offer us—a free spirit, a clear mind, and a loving heart; taken together, they operate to produce a noble life. Schweitzer himself always credited his success to what other people had done for him all life long, even though what they did for him included no grand design for his life or plan for his future. He was certain that the quality of all life in this world depended upon the love and wisdom of people. He realized that he had gotten much of both all along the way and, as his life drew to a close, he was able to rest easy with the knowledge that he had also given much and, therefore, lived very well indeed.

In his later years he expressed it this way:

> *I look back upon my youth and realize how so many people gave me help, understanding, courage—very important things to me—and they never knew it. They entered into my life and became powers within me. All of us live spiritually by what others have given us, often unwittingly, in the significant hours of our life. At the time these significant hours may not even be perceived. We may not recognize them until years later when we look back, as one remembers some long-ago music or a boyish landscape. We all owe others so much of gentleness or wisdom that we have made our own, and we may well ask ourselves what will others owe to us.*

It seems to me it would be very sad indeed to realize as we reach the end of our days that nobody owes us much of anything.

Schweitzer was German by birth, but both Germany and France claimed him as their own. This contention comes from the fact that he was born in Alsace, a province that has switched hands many times before at last being permanently annexed by France following World War II. Alsace was part of Germany when Schweitzer was born and raised there. And though German, it was not an area caught up in the rampant German nationalism of the time, which led so many of Schweitzer's generation down the narrow path to super-race mentality and glorification of military conquest. He received a fine classical education at the University of Strasbourg, the kind of education that prepares the individual for creating a life rather than merely earning a living. He was, however, very well prepared to enter any number of lucrative professions, a young man clearly headed for success. But as it turned out, his idea of success was nothing like what others had anticipated for him. When he turned his back on all the opportunities that the world had to offer, disappointing and confusing all who loved him so well, he opened himself up to a new world of opportunity that would make him one of the most loved people in the world.

He was not one of those people who, unable to cope with the challenges of the civilized world, packs off to some God-forsaken wilderness to escape responsibility. He went to Africa to make more of his life in the best possible way—by contributing more to the lives of others.

While traveling through Africa as a young man, he was overwhelmed by the untouched splendor of the place and the natural harmony that existed between all the many forms of life, human, animal, and vegetable. The innocence and simplicity of the natives also appealed to his soul. It seemed like paradise to him. What better place to preserve? What more deserving people to care for? The magnitude of its beauty and simplicity easily overpowered any fears for his own personal security or comfort. In other words, young Schweitzer fell in love in the best possible way: he fell in love with life itself. His commitment was to preserve its purity and to encourage its possibility.

Unlike so many other medical missionaries, he set no price on his service, not offering to heal their bodies in exchange for stewardship of their minds. He had no interest in converting the natives to his religion but respected their ways and always encouraged them to grow and prosper within the framework of their natural instincts. He was himself a devoted Lutheran and remained so all his life. But that was his personal preference. He was content with it. Content enough to allow others to find their own contentment.

When we think of Schweitzer, we tend to romanticize our view of the man, seeing him only as a compassionate medical missionary laboring in the jungles with natives that the rest of the world had little time for. He was all of that, and did all of that. But he was also a very successful and practical businessman. And that is worthy of comment, because it proves that there is no natural barrier between compassion and business, and no excuse for those of us who have to make money for not also providing a good and meaningful service, and doing it with dignity.

Schweitzer founded and operated a superb hospital at Lambaréné in French Equatorial Africa, now known as Gabon. It became a remarkably well-endowed institution and attracted the services of superb medical and nonmedical personnel, and the good will and good services of governments of every political stripe. This is not just because of Schweitzer's idealism, but also because of his skill as a diplomat, a recruiter, and a fund-raiser.

He was never interested in money for the sake of money. His was an entirely idealistic commitment, but he knew that ideals come to actualization through use of money, and in the case of very high ideals, lots of money. So he went out and got it. Unlike so many people who call themselves idealists, he did not delude himself into loathing money or shrink from the necessity of conducting his affairs in a businesslike manner. He did not see the spiritual/idealistic and the material/practical as two different things, but as two aspects of the same thing: successful living. Because of this, he was able to approach his work with good practical sense and make something out of his dreams.

In his lifetime this man generated millions for his work. He himself lived very well, because he lived as he chose to live—at peace with himself, in good service to the world, and in good health till his death at the age of ninety. Few people can boast such a life.

His compassion for the African natives that he served was great and unending. Hardly anyone who observed their helplessness in the face of poverty and disease would fail to be touched deeply. But few would bring themselves to do a great deal about it, and hardly anyone would give his life to their care and advancement.

What moved Albert Schweitzer to do that was something that eclipsed normal human compassion, the sort that views with alarm and then forgets in haste. It was a passionate belief in the dignity of life in all its forms, and that the honoring of every form of life was our primary purpose, ordained by God to be so. The world would never know peace until humanity accepted this divine obligation. Any individual, such as Schweitzer himself who saw this so clearly, had to act on it or perish. He did not try to convert the world to this point of view by preaching about it or by writing about it. He was out to serve his own soul first. And the way to do this was not to convert the world, but to follow his own conscience in spite of all the temptations of the world.

He has been described as a "renaissance man raised to spiritual dimensions." The designation of renaissance man refers to his wide-ranging expertise as a concert organist and music historian, philosopher, theologian, New Testament scholar, and, of course, medical missionary. He was raised, or raised himself, to spiritual dimensions because he devoted his total being to serving his highest ideal, which was the reverence for life in all its forms, at all times, and in all circumstances.

In the conduct of all our human activities and in the pursuit of all our objectives, we are obliged to consider, first and foremost, Is this consistent with the well-being of all? Does it help someone without harming anyone? Does it destroy in order to create? Although it is true that life must end in order for new life to begin, it is not our proper function to force either an end or a beginning.

Schweitzer's philosophy is deceptively simple. It is based upon only one vital concept: reverence for life.

Our culture is a fragile structure. Its integrity depends on the good will of the human race, because only human intelligence can control it and protect it. Therefore it is the sacred obligation of people to do this. Schweitzer

called this the *ethical imperative,* and said that we experience God only as we exercise the will to re-create God
as Life in the universe.

We can see God in nature as the impersonal force that
is always automatically making all things new through a
natural creative process at work within all things. But we
can experience God, that is, feel the Divine Presence and
be led to our fulfillment, only by cooperating with the
natural creative process in, as, and through all things.

This means something more than simply not killing
each other, not wantonly slaying animals or destroying the
world's vegetation. It means actively working to heal people, to educate them, to protect them from oppression,
and to teach them how to improve their approach to life's
basic functions. It has nothing to do with winning them
over to a religion or a cause or a social system created
by and for someone else at some other time and in some
other place. It has to do with accepting people as they are
and supporting their interests as they are able to conceive
of them.

It means using all of Earth's natural resources, but not
abusing them. It means replacing that which we must use:
restocking our game, replanting our forests. It means not
polluting our streams and oceans and the air we breathe.
We have a right to use all of these things, but we have an
obligation to protect them as well. Of all living creatures,
we alone have the intelligence to do this well.

To the degree that we ignore this ethical imperative, we
contribute to our own demise. We will not destroy the
world, but we will destroy ourselves by making a world
that will no longer support our existence. Life will go on,

but without us. We have no real power over Life Itself. But we have total dominion over our own lives and the world that sustains our living.

Schweitzer was an idealist, but by no means a fool. He was well aware that the governments and private corporations that so generously funded his work at Lambaréné were in no way disposed to a reverence for human life on the scale of his philosophy. In fact, they often lent themselves to the destruction of life if it seemed to serve their purpose to do so.

This did not prevent the good man from taking whatever value he could get from them: their money and whatever technical assistance or good publicity they had to offer. Nor did he preach revolution or call for their downfall. After all, he preached a philosophy of reverence for *all* life and was committed to a policy of healing error, not punishing or destroying the erroneous. This world has too often witnessed the pulling down of one offensive system only to see it immediately replaced by another system that is equally offensive and often less capable. Governments are not really the problem. Corporations are not what need to be educated. Governments and corporations are only made up of people and are always supported by popular opinion. The change that must be made is a change in the way people think and look at life, at themselves and others, at God. This kind of change requires patience and love and good example. Schweitzer's life was the epitome of all three.

Although a staunch Lutheran, Schweitzer was by no means bound to a strict Lutheran theology or indeed by mainstream Christian theology of any shading. He worked out his own belief system and wrote about it extensively, focusing particularly on the role of Paul and the meaning of Jesus. He came up with conclusions that in another age would have led him straight to the rack and the stake. Even in this century these ideas would have brought a storm of abuse down upon most people who dared to express them. But Schweitzer suffered little abuse for his views, possibly because he was not a very good target. The greatness of his work placed him in highest regard the world over. An attack on him would surely backfire, and since religious persecutors have always been a cowardly lot by definition, he was left alone. Not only would he have easily survived such an attack, but his views would have become more widely known and certainly more widely accepted by thinking people.

To Schweitzer, Jesus was an historical figure who believed that the world was on the brink of destruction because of the wickedness of mankind. His purpose was not to save the world but to so purify the souls of his people that they would survive the destruction of the world and enter a new kind of life on a new plane of existence.

His premise was wrong, of course, but his instincts were correct. God was not going to destroy the world because of human wickedness. There was nothing wrong with the world. The problem then as now was in the consciousness of the human race. The effort of Jesus to purify the consciousness of humanity was a noble one, and would lead us into a life of peace in the world.

Schweitzer believed that the right point was made by Jesus, but was lost upon Paul. Paul, a sincere follower, got caught up in the search for temporal power, and he was devoted to the idea of controlling people's behavior rather than raising their consciousness. Paul was, of course, the real founder of the Christian church, and as Christianity developed and spread, it lost track of its original purpose. It made Jesus an object of worship by claiming he was God. In doing so, it made it impossible to follow the true teachings of Jesus because, of course, no one can be as good as God.

The teachings of Jesus were quite simple, as Schweitzer perceived them. They were not really any different from his own ethical imperative, calling only for a reverence for all life, a love for self and God and one's neighbor, a forgiveness of all sin, and a lifelong commitment to learn how to manage all this in one's personal life and in the face of all the temptations of the world.

If we view Jesus in this light, he would cease to be the personality that separates Christianity from Judaism, Islam, and all the other major religions of the world. He would instead represent the idea that would unify all the religions in purpose and harmony. The truth he sought is common to all religions and is what the soul of humankind is so passionately searching for.

None of us want to go to the African wilderness and spend our lives ministering to the sick. Few of us are equipped to do so, and most of us would be more of a hindrance than a help. But all of us want to be true to the creative urgings of our own souls. All of us want to feel that whatever we spend our lives doing amounts to a life well spent. Albert Schweitzer achieved this. That is why we are drawn to him with so much admiration. The example of his life is his real gift to the world.